The Unheavenly Haven of Harlem,

1880-1935

By Daniel Agostinelli

Daniel Agostinelli
New York – Arizona – USA
623-518-2470 – agostinellidaniel@yahoo.com
Copyright © 2011 by Daniel Agostinelli – All rights reserved

There were several major ethnic and racial groups living in East Harlem at the turn of the century that practiced various religions. Protestantism was practiced by many white Anglo-Saxon immigrants including Irish immigrants and others, such as the Blacks. Blacks mainly belonged to the Baptist and Methodist denominations or followed the occult. Catholicism was practiced by many people of different ethnic and racial groups. This essay will focus on the variations practiced by the Irish Catholics and the Italian Catholics in East Harlem. Judaism will be explored for an understanding of the impact of Reform Judaism, Conservative Judaism and Orthodox Judaism. The purpose of this essay is to show how the various religions were the focal point of each group, and how each group had to adjust the manner in which they practiced their religions in order to be accepted as Americans in their new environment. The essay will also show how the various groups introduced forms of the social gospel. In addition it will explain how the various groups were able to provide each individual with an identity which defined his role within the larger community of Harlem between 1880 and 1935.

In order to understand the religious events that occurred in Harlem, between 1860 and 1935 it is important to define the boundaries of Harlem and describe the groups and populations living there in that period. East Harlem's boundaries extended from 5th Avenue in the west, to the East River in-the east; from the Harlem River in the north, to 96th Street in the south. It consisted of 200 city blocks, with tenement houses and no play areas for children, except for streets. Harlem's residents, prior to 1900, were either native-born or of West European ancestry. Irish and German influence ended during the first decade of the 20th century when Italians, Russian Jews and Blacks made their first major incursions into Harlem. Between 1900 and 1910, Irish and German population decreased by approximately one-half. (Jeffrey S. Gurock, When Harlem Was Jewish. 1870-1939 (New York: Columbia University Press, 1979), p. 50) The population between 1890 and 1900 consisted of 160,000 people who were predominantly German and Irish. By 1910, with increased immigration, other ethnic and racial groups increased the population of East Harlem to 268,021, of which, 69,266 were Italians. (Robert Whitney Peebles, Leonard Covello: A Study of Immigrant's Contribution to N.Y.C. Volume I (New York: New York University, 1967), p. 78) Between 1900 and 1914, many Italians moved into Harlem along with the Russian Jews. They formed the majority of the ethnic groups in this section by 1910. From 1910-1920, the Italian population decreased from 69,266 to 41,383--a loss of 40.3 percent, for at least 3 reasons. First, there was a drop in immigration during the war years from 1915-1919. Second, some Italian immigrants during that period returned to Italy. Third, Italians moved out of East Harlem to the outlying districts after having saved enough money to do so. Their children matured and were better educated. They wanted to own their own houses and live in a less congested area with more American neighbors. (Peebles, p. 79)

Italians were self-segregated in their enclave east of 3rd Avenue. By 1910, 59,200 Italians relocated to East Harlem, east of 3rd Avenue and South of 125th Street, except for an area from 99th Street to 104th Street, between 1st and 3rd Avenues, which was where Jews dominated. Approximately 13,000 Italians lived elsewhere in Harlem. (Gurock, p. 50)

Black settlement also occurred in Harlem between 1900 and 1910. Harlem's Black neighborhood was established in the northern parts of Central and East Harlem after 1905. Harlem at that time had 22,900 Black residents and 2/3's lived in a neighborhood bordered by 133rd to 140th Streets, between Park and Lenox Avenues, with 50 % of their population between 5th and Lenox Avenues until after World War I. The Black population then made a major movement into the predominantly Jewish sections of Lower Central and East Harlem. (Gurock, p. 50)

It is important to briefly describe what historical factors contributed to the development of Harlem. In 1658, Governor Peter Stuyvesant made an offer to whites to settle in the Northern region of Manhattan. He offered to provide one clergyman for every 25 families that settled there. They named the village New Haarlem. Later the "New" was dropped and it was called Haarlem, then finally

Harlem. The people there needed to trade with New Amsterdam. Therefore, Stuyvesant used Blacks to build a wagon road to Harlem, by developing an old Indian path, which is present day Broadway. The Harlem outpost grew. Whites lived there in luxurious houses with slaves as domestic workers. (Warren J. Halliburton and Ernest Kaiser, Harlem (New York: Doubleday & Company Inc., 1974), p. 13) Also, new pioneers came from Europe. The Dutch, German, English, French and Swiss settled on the outskirts of the new community. (Halliburton, p. 14) Some free Blacks lived there also. After 1710, whites wanted Blacks suppressed so new laws were enacted restricting their freedom. In the 1840's the fertility of the agricultural land was worn out through constant use. Many of the rich owners moved off their land and poor Irish immigrants moved in. (Halliburton, p. 17) They created shantytowns of makeshift living quarters. They raised animals and vegetables. Then the New York and Harlem Railroad began running trains from -lower Manhattan to- Harlem. In 1853 the 3rd Avenue line started its horse-drawn train. The horse-drawn train took an hour and twenty minutes to travel from lower Manhattan to Harlem. (Roi Ottley and William J. Weatherby, The Negro in New York (New York: Oceana Publications, Inc-., 1967), p. 181) It began opposite City Hall; it switched to a locomotive train at 42nd Street and it went up to 129th Street. Another means of transportation was The Harlem Navigation Line, which operated boats on the Hudson River. It could make the trip from Peck Slip to Harlem in an hour. (Ottley, p. 181) Then in 1878, 3 more railroad lines were started. (Halliburton, p. 18) Travel time was cut to 40 minutes. More sanitation facilities were installed along with lighting and communications. Brownstones were built and apartment houses. By 1890 Harlem contained most of the houses that are there today. (Halliburton, p. 19)

Harlem was transformed into an upper middle class suburb. Older immigrants found Harlem desirable. The Irish settled with Germans in East Harlem. By the 1890's Italians and Jewish immigrants settled into the cheap four and five story apartment buildings. (Halliburton, p. 19) In 1894 a rapid transit act provided for construction of a subway system which led to the development of real estate. (Gurock, p. 32)

The promise of improved transportation caused real estate to develop in Harlem. The value of real estate increased because the elevated railroad would decrease travel time to downtown Manhattan to just 30 minutes. New houses were built in anticipation of the new railroad 4 and 5 years before it was to be completed. Consequently no one was buying the buildings and people were unwilling to pay the high rents that landlords had hoped they would. The Lenox Avenue subway was finally completed in 1905. Landlords no longer cared. They were losing money and were only interested in selling their empty apartments. (Halliburton, p. 20) They then sold to anyone who was interested. At the turn of the century the many people migrating to America and the Black people that were migrating to northern cities were able to take advantage of the situation in Harlem.

The Pilgrims and the Puritans were very significant in the development of the United States. Their ideology emphasized the Protestant faith, which stressed hard work and individual accomplishment. They admired the striving for wealth, cherished the Anglo-Saxon system and heritage, and the written compact. They brought with them the English language; they laid the foundation for American society. All immigrant groups that came after them had to absorb this culture to be accepted as Americans. (Leonard Dinnerstein and David M. Reimers, Ethnic Americans (New York: Harper & Row, Publishers, 1988), p. 5)

There were many Protestant denominations in America. Some of the Irish, like some of the Germans, were Protestants who belonged to Lutheran or reformed churches, many were Methodist and Baptist who left their home for religious and economic reasons; they attended their own churches, and they prospered in the New World. Many were Presbyterians, whose doctrine in contemporary America most closely resembled the Puritans, who frowned on dancing, card playing, the theater and breaking the Sabbath or engaging in any frivolous pastimes. The New World loosened Old World ties and some people deviated from them and behaved inappropriately, they fiddled, sang, reveled, raced horses, gambled, and got drunk and fought. (Dinnerstein, pp. 7, 8)

What was important about East Harlem was that some of the major religious groups underwent or began to undergo a transformation of their traditional structures. This change was catalyzed by modern liberal notions of some Protestant groups in America who were the creators of a new American tradition, defining its interests and values. Any ethnic or racial group that entered the United States had to model themselves according to those Protestant notions to be accepted by the nativist as Americans.

The Protestants believed in the social gospel, whereby man should work, make money and give it to the poor. (Moses Rischin, The Promised City '(Massachusetts: Harvard University Press, 1962), p. 197) However, their philanthropy was not meant so much to help the poor as it was to instill in the immigrants their own "notions of what Americanism is and should be. It will be shown that they hated the immigrant's ritualistic religious observances, finding them to be a threat to their values and interests.

German Jews, who were established in America earlier in the 19th century, continued to modernize their traditional order which had begun in Germany. They moved away from their traditional practices in Harlem and had the effect of making them appear like the liberal Protestants both physically and religiously. They threw off some of their religious oppressive and ritualistic practices to assume a more liberal form of dress and religion. It was easier for German Jews to be accepted in America, because of their physical likeness to many WASPs, they had white skin, blond hair, blue eyes, etc. (Stephen Birmingham, The Rest Of Us (Massachusetts. Little, Brown and Company, 1984), p. 15) They created organizations to modernize their Jewish co-religionists partly out of their obligation as good Jews. Also they had a self-serving interest in stifling anti-Semitism, which was already present and they were afraid would increase. They feared it would have an impact on their business enterprises. (Birmingham, p. 14) These Protestant notions had an interesting effect on the various immigrant and racial groups in East Harlem. Its effect on the Jews and Italians, as will be explained, was that in order for them to assimilate into the American culture, the Jews had to move away from their traditional roots, and the Italian Catholics, by contrast, had to move into the traditional Catholic Church in order to be respected by the Irish Catholics as Americans. (Dinnerstein, p. 57)

The arrival of poor immigrants from Europe caused a reaction in America known as the nativist movement. The United States had been a country of immigrants all along. Many enjoyed a common Puritan and Anglo-Saxon background of militant middle-class liberalism. The majority were descended from similar ancestors speaking the same language, practicing the same religion and the same principles of government. (Erik Amfitheatrof, The Children of Columbus (Boston: Little, Brown and Company, 1973), p. 102) The original Americans became "old" Americans, or "old stock", or "white Anglo-Saxon

Protestants". Those who were most like them could join them easily. It was important to be white, of British origin and Protestant. If one was all three, then one either was not an immigrant or one would be an immigrant for a short period of time. It depended on how close you were to this description. Germans were placed above the Irish because they were more competent craftsmen and farmers. Even though Germans spoke a different language they were thought to be closer to the WASP ideal than English-speaking Catholic and Celtic Irish. It was for this reason that the German Jews who arrived in the 1840's and 1850's were more easily assimilated. Their physical characteristics were closely linked with the Germans. (Nathan Glazer and Daniel Patrick Moynihan, Beyond the Melting Pot (Massachusetts: The M.I.T. Press, 1963), pp. 15, 16)

The first group that will be explored is the Jewish East European immigrants, both Russian and Polish that arrived between 1881 and 1915 seemed inadaptable. The East European Jews seemed threatening to the reputation of German Jews; they had a religious tradition that the older-established German Jews considered barbaric. (Birmingham, p. 9)

Beginning 1906, nearly ninety thousand Jews arrived in New York City every year, mostly from Russia and Poland. The Jewish population came close to a million in that year. (Birmingham, p. 15) By 1915 the population was a million and a half; they were massed together on the Lower East Side and were very conspicuous. They were poor, hungry, ill clothed, and sickly and some were illiterate, speaking no English. (Birmingham, p. 9) They looked like hobos with gunny sacks, swarthy skinned, bearded and side-curled, constantly in need of baths and fumigation. They looked, and were, frightened, fearful, defiant and suspicious; however, they were not beggars. (Birmingham, p. 16) They were proud, feisty, independent and argumentative. Their names were unpronounceable and they spoke Yiddish, which sounded like German, but was written in Hebrew characters, backward; from right to left. The German Jews criticized their Yiddish language as a "vulgar jargon". (Birmingham, p. 17) The Jew who arrived in New York hated to be called a "greenhorn." He was wearing a long beard, little black cap, and carried wears in his push-cart. When he prayed his head was covered by a black and white praying-shawl, and a cube of the phylactery was attached to his forehead and left arm. The cubes were fastened by two straps of goat skin, black and white; those on the forehead hung down and those attached to the other cube were wound seven times around the left arm. Inside each cube was a white parchment on which was written the Hebrew word for God, which must never be spoken by a Jew. (Hutchins Hapgood, The Spirit of the Ghetto. (Massachusetts: Harvard University Press, 1967), p. 13) The old immigrants were entirely ignorant of modern culture; they were submerged in an old outworn tradition. (Hapgood, p. 17) The newspapers described the East European Jews as ignorant, primitive and the dregs of society. They lived in filthy tenements, with vermin, garbage, marital disorders, insanity, violence, gangs, alcoholism, starvation, prostitution and crime. The East European Jews were giving the German Jews a bad name by association and threatening their hard acquired Americanization. (Birmingham, p. 17)

Arrival in America shocked and disrupted the East European Jews, especially those who had remained religious. In Eastern Europe it was possible within the shtetl to keep old traditions and rituals. In Europe secular enlightenment had an affect on rabbinical authority, but it was not destroyed. However, in America, their religion did not play an official role, as it did in Europe. The dominant faith in America was Protestantism, which was threatening and strange to the Jews. German Jews, wanting to be accepted as Americans, had found it necessary to turn away from their old religious traditions. (Irving Howe, World of Our Fathers (New York: Simon & Schuster, Inc., 1976), p. 99)

East European Jews found that the observance of the Sabbath, in America, was violated. Shopkeepers stood in their shops and peddlers shouted their wares. Everywhere there was disbelief. The conservative and reform congregations, formed earlier by the acculturated German Jews threatened the interest and values of the East European Jews. (Howe, p. 99)

The rabbi's authority was being undermined in America. According to the American custom a rabbi was not taken by a synagogue for more than a year at a time. In contrast to Europe he would have been there for life. In addition, his son or son-in-law would assume his place after he died. (Howe, p. 99) In Russia, the rabbi was a great person; he remained a rabbi all his life, and the only rabbi in the town. In America, they judged whether or not a rabbi was good. If they wanted him, they kept him, if not, they threw him out. (Howe, p. 96) The Jews belonged to one congregation with one cantor. The rabbi, in Russia, was full of learning and piety, always respected and supported by the congregation. The members of the congregation were taxed on meat, salt and other foods for his sustenance. In contrast to Russia, the East European Jews had many congregations on the Lower East Side, almost one on every street. When they moved north to Harlem they carried their customs with them. Jews came from different cities in Europe. In New York they had a different congregation to represent each different city in East Europe; consequently, they were small, poor and unimportant and could not pay the rabbi a regular salary. The Rabbi instead received occasional fees for his services at weddings, births and holy festivals. The result was a falling-off in the character of the rabbis. In East Harlem rabbis were not learned men who knew the Talmud by heart. They did not have degrees from the rabbinical colleges; they had instead other worldly motives. Rabbis were selected for knowing a little about the contents of the Talmud, they were said by some to be good for nothing.

They wore high hats and were called fake rabbis only interested in business. (Howe, p. 99) There was a lack of qualified rabbis to officiate at marriages. In the instance of the death of a married man before his wife had conceived or bore a child, the man's brother had an obligation to marry the widow after a period of 3 months required by rabbinic decree. Some rabbis would permit the marriage without the waiting period. This made the children of such a union illegitimate. (Howe, p. 97) Unqualified ritual slaughterers, kosher butchers and supervising rabbis compounded the problem. In Harlem Jews were eating meat that was not killed properly. The slaughter houses employed an orthodox Jew, who was not a rabbi, to see-that the-meat was properly killed; they were doing it wrong. (Hapgood, p. 66) Housewives, mainly interested in cheaper prices for food, bought their meat and were satisfied that the meat was kosher because it was advertised as such; they had no guarantee that it was.

Jews were confused by the gentiles who prayed to a personal god for personal needs, and who would give heed to such prayers. To the Jews prayer was used to placate god; prayers were done automatically as was prescribed. (Howe, p. 97) In New York all this was different and it bothered many unacculturated Jews who wanted to remain rooted in the traditional structure of Judaism. (Howe, p. 99) The traditional patterns of deference and respect were broken; a part of religious life was violated. (Howe, p. 96) They believed that there was no place for them in America.

(Howe, p. 93)

In order for East European Jews to be accepted in America they had to learn English and change their style of clothes. They had to wear a short coat instead of a long one. Women had to discard their wigs, which were strictly required by the orthodox in Russia, (the equivalent of a man shaving off his beard) they had to go to the synagogue with their natural hair. (Hapgood, p. 17) They needed .to have the appearance of the WASP, who was the model American.

A minority of the Jewish women in Harlem were very modern. They were educated and had economic ideas about labor and capital. They were accused as having masculine virtues, being straightforward and intensely serious. (Hapgood, p. 77) They were insulted if men were too polite when speaking or working with hem. They had lost their faith in the orthodox religion. They became dentists, physicians, writers, lawyers. They directed the careers of their husbands, requiring them to become doctors or lawyers or be jilted. (Hapgood, p. 79) The acculturated Jewish women viewed American women as. uninterested in great principles, being frivolous, incapable of devotion to persons or movements, reading books only for amusement, caring~ nothing for real literature. (Hapgood, p. 82) American women, they claimed, cared only for what was pretty or charming and practical; they cared nothing for poetry - and beauty and essential humanity. (Hapgood, p. 83)

The German Jews had started out as peddlers a generation earlier. When they did business they concluded it with a handshake. The Russians, by contrast, were noisy, brash, and assertive. When unhappy about the price of an item, they beat their breast and wailed to make their point. (Birmingham, p. 19) The German Jews wanted to disown their spiritual cousins, but, some argued that the Talmudic principles of righteousness obligated the uptown German Jews to help the East European Jews downtown. (Birmingham, p. 20) The German Jews, like the Protestants, believed in the social gospel. The solution was to try to reshape- these shabby people. The United Hebrew Charities began providing free lodging, meals, medical care and counseling for the new immigrants, along with lectures, classes teaching English and American morals, manners, modes of dress and dangers of socialism. (Birmingham, p. 21) German Jewish businessmen established small-loan societies to help immigrants get loans to establish businesses other than pushcart vending. (Birmingham, p. 22)

Julia Richman, an acculturated German Jew, lived at 330 Central Park West in an affluent ghetto located west of Central Park, which was a wealthy German-Jewish residential district of the Upper West Side. The neighborhood contained large apartment houses with elevators, with high ceilings, scenic views of the city and servants' rooms. (Birmingham, p. 11) Julia Richman wanted to help the East European Jews. The German-Jews had been poor immigrants a generation earlier, during and after the Civil War. They too, like East European Jews began in business as foot peddlers and later went into banking, retailing and manufacturing. Guggenheim, Lehman, Straus, Sachs, Altman, Loeb and Seligman were some of the most prominent businessmen living in that wealthy section of West Harlem. (Birmingham, p. 12)

Protestant patricians, like the acculturated German Jews, were reformers. They were men of wealth and executives in high positions. Protestant churchmen accepted the theory of evolution and liberalized religious thought; they embraced the social gospel. (Rischin, p. 197) The Protestants4 like the Catholics and Jews cared for the less fortunate as a religious obligation. -The German Jewish immigrants joined the reformers. They all singled out the East European Jews to be brought within the fold of the community. Older East European Jewish immigrants suspected that the reformers were trying to convert them to Christianity. (Rischin, p. 199)

Wealthy Protestant Christian ladies and Julia Richman, a German Jew, visited the Lower East Side. They gave Christian charity to the poor East European Jews. The Protestant ladies were distrusted. They were suspected of being missionaries bent on conversion of the Jews to Christianity. The motive of Julia Richman, like the wealthy Protestant ladies of Harlem, was self-serving and based on embarrassment. She was trying to impose her own modern values on the East European Jews. On the other hand the

East Europeans had standards of their own which required less change. Julia was viewed by them to be a capitalist who traditionally oppressed the poor. Also, she represented a form of Judaism that East Europeans did not accept. She was actually practicing a religion different from their own. (Birmingham p. 14)

In order to understand the position of the East European Jews it is important to understand what occurred one generation earlier. In 1853, the only major transportation from the Lower East Side to Harlem was the Third Avenue horse-car lines. (Gurock, p. 7) At first, after the Civil War, and again in the 1880's, many German-Jewish merchants left the Lower East Side and moved north to Harlem. (Gurock, p. 18)   When the German Jews arrived in America their numbers were small and unnoticed. During the Civil War they gained fortunes of their own. In- 1870 there were only eighty thousand Jews in New York City. They did not threaten Christian society with their ways since they worked hard and gained a reputation for probity. (Birmingham, p. 15) German Jews had acquired money and were able to escape the downtown overcrowded ghetto to take advantage of commercial opportunities uptown. They built their homes within Harlem's Third Avenue commercial district. (Gurock, p. 7) They settled in lower Harlem, as section North of Central Park at 110th Street to 145th Street, and East of Morningside Park and St. Nicholas Park on the West Side in the 1890's. (Gurock, p. 6) After vacating the Lower East

Side, they, along with the Irish and German Americans, were replaced by Russian-Jews and Italian immigrants. (Gurock, p. 18)

During the 1880's Harlem became populated because of improved transportation system. The extension of the Second and Third Avenue railroads to the northern tip of Manhattan; occurred in 1879 and 1880 respectively. Travel time between Harlem and City Hall was cut nearly in half. (Gurock, pp. 14, 15) After 1881, the lines were finished and the new immigrants from Eastern Europe entered the new residential areas in Harlem. The Lower East Side had become crowded and it was unable to absorb the new immigrants from Eastern. Europe. In 1894, a rapid transit act provided for construction of a subway system which led to the development of real estate. (Gurock, p. 32) The transit act, as was stated earlier, convinced real estate operators to begin developing Harlem by building tenements, brownstone flats and private homes; focusing primarily upon those properties near the elevated lines. (Gurock, pp. 14, 15)

However, legal and financial problems delayed construction of the transit system. Harlem then had newly constructed housing and no one to occupy it. (Gurock, p.32) So along 7th and Lenox Avenues in the streets from 130 to 140's, luxurious apartments were- built around 1900 in West Harlem. (Osofsky p. 89) Many of the buildings were equipped with elevators, maid's rooms and butler's quarters. The excitement led to overbuilding of apartments. Vacancies could not be filled. Rents which had been too high dropped as landlords competed for tenants. (Osofsky, p. 90) Realtors became fearful that they would lose their investments and began to grant terms of free rent to attract prospective tenants. Competition to fill their vacancies caused landlords to have a rent war. (Gurock, p. 32) It was during this period that thousand of Russian-Jews moved uptown in anticipation of getting greater privacy in their living quarters and the possibility of becoming a landlord. (Gurock, p. 33)

Although in 1890 there were East European Jews living in Harlem, mass migration did not occur until 1895 after the Metropolitan Street Railway Company built an overhead trolley from Battery Park to Central Park West; it had been completed in the 1890's. It extended eastward across 116th Street through Central Harlem; this made it possible for Harlemites to travel downtown for a 5 cent fare. (Gurock, p. 32) The East European Jews moved into the Lower East Side as thousands of German Jews moved cut of the downtown ghetto when rapid transit lines reached uptown. (Gurock, p. 3)

Reform Judaism was introduced in Harlem by the acculturated German Jews. German Jews, living in Harlem, realized they could not rely upon downtown institutions for their own spiritual inspiration and religious leadership. They still wanted to pray on Sabbaths and Holidays as they did in their former synagogues. They did not want to travel 5 miles downtown to the Lower East Side to attend them.

They then decided to build their own Harlem synagogue, along with its own burial grounds, a Hebrew school and social center. (Gurock, p. 9)

Jewish synagogues bought property in the neighborhood. This section became known as "Little Russia". (Osofsky, p. 88) The German Jewish businessmen had tailored their religion to fit the Protestant mode. (Birmingham p.14) The German Jews practiced Reform Judaism; they believed that reason should be used over blind and bigoted faith. (Birmingham, pg. 13) The atmosphere in the Reform Temple was indistinguishable from an American Protestant church. East Europeans viewed this as shocking. They feared that their faith could erode in America if they were not watchful. (Birmingham, p. 14)

In Harlem at the turn of the 20th century, there was a Reform movement in Judaism. North American Jews, along with Jews in other countries, (sometimes using different names) identified themselves as members of Orthodox, Conservative, Reform or Reconstructionist movements. These movements were not different denominations but were different philosophies. It is important to note that there is also a wide diversity in custom, practice and observances within each of these movements. Here is a brief overview of each of the movements as they existed in Harlem. (Stephen J. Einstein, Every Person's Guide to Judaism (New York: UAHC Press, 1989), p. 151)

The Reform movement was the most liberal approach to Judaism. It arose in Germany as the response to the modern world. In the 19th century Jews entered into activities that were once closed to them. They believed that Judaism was antiquated and not in keeping with the modern age. As a result they looked for a means of reconciling Jewish beliefs with the modern world. The modern Reformist believed, unlike the Orthodox, that religion is organic and dynamic; it changes and meets with each changing situation. The Reformists eliminated all ideas that were deemed outmoded. (Einstein, p. 153)

Some of the reforms made, in Harlem, were in the worship service. English was used instead of Hebrew. The service was shortened. Reformers began a weekly sermon as a way of educating the community about the basic teachings of Judaism. Another innovation was the inclusion of a Friday evening service, rather than a brief service at sundown. German Jews no longer prayed for the advent of a personal Messiah, instead they prayed for a Messianic Age. They stopped prayers for the reestablishment of the ancient Temple and the practice of married women ritually immersing themselves after their menstrual period. (Einstein, p. 153)

The Reform Jews studied their religious practices and continued those which they deemed meaningful. They did not believe that every word in the Torah comes directly from God; it is instead believed to be a record of the events that occurred between the people and God. The Reform movement placed a major emphasis on the autonomy of the individual and his absolute right to follow his own conscience. (Einstein p. 154)

The social gospel was practiced within the Reform movement. The Reform movement insisted that the essence of Judaism is its ethical teaching. This belief motivated them to become active in human rights struggles and other forms of social action. They were committed to equality of the sexes, with boys and girls receiving the same education and women receiving leadership roles in the synagogues; including the ordination of women as rabbis and cantors. (Einstein, p. 154)

Initially Reform Jews did not observe the dietary laws or support the establishment of a Jewish state. Men worshiped without wearing skullcaps or prayer shawls and Hebrew use at services was minimal. (Einstein, p. 154)

Harlem's first synagogue was started by Jewish businessmen in 1869 who began meeting for Sabbath and Holiday services at the Harlem Savings Bank at 124th Street and Third Avenue. The early leaders were Marcus Marx, a hatter and clothier, Israel Stone, a clothier; brothers Samuel and Gershom Boehm, liquor dealers and a jeweler named Isaac Peiser; this led to the formation of Congregation Hand-in-Hand in 1873 with 12 charter members. However, growth of membership was slow due to disputes over the synagogue's ritual practices. The synagogue, though Orthodox, broke a religious tradition by allowing women to sit with the men. Also in 1877 a radical break with Orthodoxy was made by allowing an organ into the synagogue, causing offended members to create their own Congregation Tents of Israel in a nearby hall. A year later a second group left causing membership to dwindle to 70 members creating such financial burden on the Congregation Hand-in-Hand that it remained weak, not able to build a sanctuary or even retain a full time cantor or rabbi. The congregation did establish a free Jewish religious school in 1876 called the Shangarai Talmud Torah of Harlem, under the leadership of the Carvalho family. (Gurock, p. 10) They purchased a cemetery plot in Bayside, New York in 1879 because the leaders were concerned with every phase of their members lives.

In order to strengthen the Jewish family and ties between neighbors in the community, the leaders believed that two institutions could be used; they established the Harlem YMHA and Harlem Lodge of the B'nai B'rith in 1879 and 1882 respectively. Religious leaders hoped that the people attending the Y and Lodge would eventually attend the religious institutions that were associated with them to bring Jews who had strayed from Judaism back into the fold. However, those same individuals were not dedicated to synagogue life. (Gurock, p. 12)

Newly settled affluent German Jews became members of Congregation Hand-in-Hand which grew and became a leading Reform religious institution in an architecturally magnificent building, the Temple Israel at 125th Street and Fifth Avenue. The congregation in 1882 purchased the Grace Episcopal Church, which it had been leasing; they were then able to hire their first full time Rabbi, Dr. Maurice Harris, who had been a student of the Emanuel Theological Seminary. (Gurock, p. 19)

Dr. Maurice Harris was an advocate of Reform practices. He inspired modifications in the Orthodox ritual of the Congregation Hand-in-Hand. He introduced more English language prayers into the service. He abandoned the Orthodox siddur (prayer book) completely in favor of English. He adopted the Union Prayer Book for use by Reform Congregations for Congregation Hand-in-Hand services. Dr. Harris was also moderate. He advocated the continued observance of the traditional religious "second holy day" of Festivals and permitted the wearing of a skullcap during services. (Gurock, p. 19)

As was mentioned earlier some members of Congregation Hand-in-Hand were traditionalist. They preferred the old ritual ways. They called for a meeting of all the members for a peace conference to reconcile the synagogue's factions. The leaders of the congregation who wanted to maintain unity, called upon worshipers to settle their differences and to Support their present executive minister. (Gurock, p. 20)

In 1888, the Reform group of Congregation Hand-in-Hand broke away and built the Temple Israel of Harlem at 125th Street and Fifth Avenue because of the growing affluent Jewish community to the West Side of Harlem. It had an impressive membership. It included the city's most important Jewish families: Daniel P. Hays, Vice-President of the Temple in 1888 and its President in 1890 whose genealogy traced to a period before the Revolutionary War. Cyrus L. Sulzburger was trustee of the congregation and chairman of its Religious School Union. Benjamin Peixotto was a noted diplomat and statesman who along with many professionals and successful businessmen financed the reform institution. The Temple Israel, in 1903 moved further west, following its most affluent members, into a newly constructed Central Harlem neighborhood at 120th Street and Lenox Avenue. (Gurock, p. 21)

The Temple Israel, under the leadership of Rabbi Harris, participated in Reform communal activities. He founded the Harlem Temple's Sisterhood of Personal Service in 1891. This midtown charitable organization, modeled after the Temple Emanuel Sisterhood, believed in the "social gospel." Following reform leaders they declared charity to be the duty of Jews, in accordance with Mosaic legislation to help in solving the prevailing social problems. The women of Temple Israel responded by organizing a Perseverance Club for working women and a kindergarten for needy tenement children. (Gurock, p. 21)

There was another faction of Jews that was less liberal. The group gave rise to a Conservative movement in Harlem when some Reformers believed that they had given up too much of their Jewish tradition. The Conservative group looked for a middle ground where more of Judaism would be conserved. The Conservatives believed that the law was not set but evolved over the course of Jewish history. Conservatives believed the law was divinely inspired, therefore binding, but the individual was free to reject aspects of Jewish tradition. Any change, they believed, in Jewish law must be decided by a special rabbinical committee. The Conservative Jews upheld the Sabbath observances and the Jewish dietary laws. (Einstein, p. 155)

The Conservatives emphasized an attachment to Jewish communities world wide. Although they were concerned with the social gospel, it was less universalistic than the Reform movement. The Conservative's educational programs taught art, music, dance, literature and Modern Hebrew along with classical Jewish studies. Boys and girls were taught the same. (Einstein, p. 155)

The arrival of other congregations to Harlem transformed it into a growing neighborhood attractive to different segments of German-Jewish society. There were Conservative-Orthodox institutions established in Harlem. Chevrah Anche Chesed, was a small German Conservative-Orthodox congregation founded in 1876 at Beekman Place near 50th Street; in 1879 it moved to Yorkville and in 1893 it migrated to Harlem. It opened its membership to all German Jews and joined with Temple Mount Zion to serve the Lower Harlem Community. Temple Mount Zion, earlier, had been established in a public hall by German and Hungarian Jews. In 1888, congregation Mount Zion changed its denomination from Orthodox to moderate

Reform. The two synagogues grew in membership, practiced the social gospel and began playing roles in Harlem social work serving both German and East European constituency. (Gurock, pp. 22, 23)

Congregation Alteres Zvi, like Anche Chesed, was a Conservative-Orthodox institution which replaced Congregation Hand-in-Hand and was the first Harlem German congregation to solicit East European members through advertisement in the Yiddishes Tageblatt. (Gurock, p. 25)

The Orthodox movement was the most traditional movement which had an impact in Harlem. According to Orthodoxy, the Torah's interpretations were divinely revealed; the laws and traditions-were of direct divine origin, they had to be followed by all who wished to do the will of God. All ritual and ethical commandments were equally binding. An infraction of any commandment was a sin. It was the Torah, and not one's personal belief or conscience that was followed. Some central governing laws were the dietary laws, observance of the Sabbath including devotion to prayer, study, rest, and visiting family and friends. No form of work can be done on the Sabbath. All services were conducted in Hebrew with no musical instruments used on Shabbat and other major holidays. In services men and women had to sit separately. The woman's domain was the home and the man's domain was the synagogue. Women were not permitted to be rabbis or to lead worship services. (Einstein, p. 152)

Within the Orthodox community there were gradations in observance and practice. The Ultra-Orthodox were the most traditional. The men wear black hats, coats, pants and white shirts, with untrimmed beards and side curls. The women dressed modestly and if married they kept their heads covered. The Orthodox Jews believed that other movements were deviations from authentic Torah-true Judaism. (Einstein p. 152)

Congregation Beth Tephilah was an Orthodox institution, a private synagogue owned and operated by a Reverend Samuel Distillator, a Russian Jew. He operated this Orthodox German congregation in several small rented halls in the 1890's. He served the community in 3 capacities. He was a Rabbi, Mesader Kedushin (performer of marriage ceremonies), and a ritual slaughterer; he advertised his talents in the Yiddish and Anglo-Jewish press. (Gurock, p. 24) In 1892 he was arrested by the Health Department for operating a butcher shop without an approved city code permit. (Gurock, p. 25) Apparently, Rabbi Distillator was an example of a rabbi that used his credentials mainly for business purposes.

The Reconstruction movement was the latest movement. The leaders wanted to keep the Jewish youth rooted in Judaism. The movement followed the teaching of Mordecai M. Kaplan. He believed that Judaism was more than a religion. He saw it as an evolving religious civilization with tradition, laws, customs, languages, literature, music, and art combining to form Judaism. He saw Israel as the hub of a wheel with religion, culture and ethics as the spokes and the diaspora as its rim. (Gurock, p.115)

The Reconstructionist rejected the idea that the Jews were the chosen people. They did not hope for the reconstruction of the Temple in Jerusalem, but instead they believed in a personal Messiah with a hope for the advent of a Messianic Era. God was not seen as supernatural. God was instead a Process of Power an expression of high values, ideals and virtues of the group. The Torah was not seen as a reflection of truth, but a reflection of the Jews' search for God. In addition Reconstructionist believe in full equality between men and women. They allow women to become rabbis as well. (Einstein, p. 156)

Mordecai Kaplan believed that modern synagogues were the key to the perpetuation of Judaism in America. A modern synagogue could be used for more than worship and sacred study. It would be a social agency providing members with a feeling of ethnic togetherness as well as a Jewish center synagogue which would sponsor youth programs, social clubs, dances and athletic events. It would bring Jewish young adults together into a synagogue where their social interest would broaden and eventually include spiritual matters. This modern synagogue represented an attempt to present Jewish traditions within an American cultural context. (Gurock, p. 115) The synagogue was the center of Jewish life. In Harlem, the Jewish center concept was developed to maintain the Jewish identification among immigrants and their children. (Gurock, pp. 116, 117)

The American Jewish community was established by American born traditional rabbis who graduated from the Jewish Theological Seminary, having learned spiritual leadership. Herbert S. Goldstein established in Harlem the Institutional Synagogue. Goldstein was a colleague of Kaplan. They were committed to reaching the acculturated Jews. (Gurock, p. 116, 117)

THE ARRIVAL OF THE EAST EUROPEAN JEW UPTOWN, 1895-1910

After the German Jews evacuated the Lower East Side, East European Jews began establishing -their own colony in Harlem. (Gurock, p. 26) East European Jews left the Lower East Side in search of better homes because Lower Manhattan became overcrowded with nearly a million people living there. (Gurock, p. 5) In 1890, 1,300 Russian Polish Jews settled in the ethnic tenement district of East Harlem and in the better Irish-German neighborhood west of Third Avenue. The East European Jews founded in 1891 their first congregation, the Nachlath Zvi, which was their first religious school. In Harlem, and one year later they founded the Uptown Talmud Torah. (Gurock, p. 26)

In 1900, a Russian-Jewish community of approximately 17,000, mainly immigrant families, was concentrated in the predominantly Irish-German East Harlem. This neighborhood located south of 110th Street and east of Lexington Avenue was a densely populated working-class tenement district. The affluent Russian Jews populated the brownstone flat and apartment house section west of Lexington Avenue. (Gurock, p. 36) Only a small number of Jews settled in East Harlem's growing "Little Italy", which was bordered by the East River and Third Avenue between 105th and 120th streets. (Gurock, p. 36)

By the 1900's Russian Jews constituted the majority of Harlem's Jewish residents. They also established communal institutions designed to serve the needs of the growing immigrant population. (Gurock, p. 26) By 1900 there was a large Jewish colony in Harlem, between 97th and 142nd streets. Harlem, a decade later, was as busy and congested as the Lower East Side. East Harlem, along Lexington Avenue between 72nd and 100th streets, became a colony for the East European Jews shortly before and after the turn of the century. (Howe, p. 131)

The migration of East European Jews from the Lower East Side to Harlem was a sign of economic and social advancement for a limited part of East European families. This Jewish group settled in Harlem after 1903 along Lenox, Madison and Fifth Avenues in spacious six and seven-story elevator apartments. The vast majority of the East European Jews from the Lower East Side migrated to Harlem in the hope of making economic progress. They wanted to escape ghetto overcrowding and obtain uptown housing which was superior to, and only slightly more expensive than, the ghetto's accommodations of the Lower East Side. Included in this migration, into Harlem, were thousands of newly arrived East European Jews which the downtown ghetto could not absorb. In 1910 there were 100,000 Jews living in several Harlem neighborhoods. (Gurock, p. 28)

In 1903 the nearly completed rapid transit system made migration of Jews intensify, from the Lower East Side, northward into Harlem. Many of the vacant apartments in Harlem were filled, creating a housing shortage. Rents began to rise. Real estate values increased. Three-story private residences in East Harlem were replaced with six-story tenements. Many Russian immigrants invested in the real estate market during this post 1903 phase of Harlem's development. (Gurock, p. 45)

In the next decade 80,000 more Russian Jews moved to Harlem supplanting the Irish and the Germans and became the dominant ethnic group south of 125th Street and west of Third Avenue. The poorer Jews lived east of Third Avenue south of "Little Italy." (Gurock, pp. 40, 41) East Harlem neighborhoods lay south of 110th Street and east of Fifth Avenue which contained most of Harlem's first Russian settlers. In 1910 it held 1/2 of Harlem's 100,000 Russian Jews. With 59 % living within Central and East Harlem immediately north and west of 110th Street and 5th Avenue. The remaining scattered north of 120th Street. (Gurock, p. 49) By 1910, Harlem was the second largest concentration of immigrant East European Jews in the United States. (Gurock, pp.40, 41)

There were two communities in Harlem; the acculturated and the unacculturated. (Gurock, p. 60) Both groups wanted to retain the ideals of European religion and community. (Gurock, p. 43) The non-acculturated Jews, who migrated to Harlem, did not move out of social choice, but out of economic necessity. (Gurock, p. 58) The unacculturated Jews wanted to maintain the goals, values and ties of the downtown ghetto in their social movements and organizations in Harlem. They were socially and psychologically unprepared for life outside their old ethnic community. (Gurock, p. 43) They wanted to build a second ghetto community rooted in European and downtown ideas and institutions. (Gurock, p. 86)

Many other Jews of Eastern Europe gloried in their separateness. They were rendered conspicuous by their religious practice and observance. Their religious ordinances governed the most minute aspects of their everyday lives and their cycles of fasts, holy days, festivals and bereavements. It supervised work, rest, dress, reading and writing, food, drink, cleanliness and health. To deviate from the slightest detail was heresy and invited ostracism. (Rischin, p. 35) They prayed three times daily affirming the magnificence of God's work, the Messianic coming, the mission of the children of Israel and the future life. Their religion caused them to seek work in industries that did not forbid the performance of religious duties, honoring the Sabbath and celebration of religious festivals. (Rischin, p. 61) Many immigrants worked in religious capacities. They became circumcisers, and ritual slaughterers. (Rischin, p. 73)

American born Jewish children strayed away from Judaism. The landsmanshaft synagogues, and cheders and the Jewish private elementary school where Jewish boys were exposed to the Hebrew language, biblical and rabbinic texts were not able to instill a love of Judaism in American-born children of immigrants. The old-world medium of their religious message was inappropriate. The cheder teacher, in Harlem, was poorly trained but provided the boys (girls were excluded) with a basic education. (Gurock, p. 90)

In Russia the boy went to the' "cheder", a school, where he learned religion and the importance of honoring his parents. He was taught that his highest ambition was to be a great scholar--to know the Bible and to serve God. He was taught to respect the aged and the rabbi. (Hapgood, pp. 21, 23)

In the old-world the intellectually promising boys would continue their education at the yeshiva, where they learned the Talmud and rabbinic texts and later they would become the leading scholars and religious leaders of Eastern European Jews. The Talmud torah, on the other hand, was a public school to educate indigent children and orphans who could not afford the cheder tuition. Talmud torah students rarely went to the yeshiva. The emphasis was on preparing them for the hostile gentile outside world. Some students were instructed in usable trades or crafts; going to the Talmud torah was humiliating. The system of cheder, yeshiva and Talmud torah placed a premium on religious learning and showed no concern with integrating with other ethnic and religious groups in the general society; this system had little chance in surviving in America. (Gurock, p. 91) Most immigrant Jews wanted their children to learn American ways. Therefore, most Jews showed little interest in perpetuating the old-world system in America. (Gurock, p. 92) Even unacculturated children showed little interest in practicing the landsmanshaft religion of their parents. The ritual practices were unintelligible to them and they had no nostalgia for the European past. (Gurock, p. 93)

In East Harlem the public school did not contain the religious element. Reading, mathematics and a little history were taught. Instruction was entirely secular. Students were encouraged to be independent and skeptical. They adapted ideas about social equality and contempt for authority. Their Jewish influences were weakened; their ceremonial life was made to be ridiculous. Children regarded their parents as greenhorn. The "chaider" (Jewish elementary school of Eastern Europe) in America assumed a position entirely subordinate. (Hapgood, p. 24) Orthodox parents began to see that in order for the boy to get along in America he had to learn business or become a doctor or lawyer. (Hapgood, p. 25)

Unaccultuated parents were concerned. They wanted to instill love for Judaism in their children. They put their children in schools in their own homes or rented lofts with untrained teachers who taught them a few prayers by rote. (Gurock, p. 93) This group kept contact with the downtown ghetto. They transplanted their downtown ghetto culture to Harlem through their communal institutions. (Gurock, p. 58) Unacculturated Jews used their old religious institutions, such as the landsmanshaft, (a synagogue of ritual practices.) self-help organizations, chevrah congregations, small cheders (schools) and European style yeshivas (attended after primary school. It provided the Jewish community with religious leaders). The ghetto downtown had served as a fortress and a prison. It provided the new immigrant with familiar Jewish surroundings in their landsmanshaft synagogues and debating clubs. It gave the immigrant a feeling of belonging in the strange American surroundings. These notions were apparent in both landsmanshaft synagogues and the ultra-Orthodox Jews who opposed the modernization taking place in the Harlem Talmud Torah movement. (Gurock, p. 59) They continued to teach old-world Judaism while Americanization made an impact on the immigrant children. The Harlem Jewish youth had not been receiving instruction in Judaism. It made them prey for Christian missionaries. (Gurock, p. 94)

Acculturated Jews, unlike the unacculturated, formed a new type of American Judaism in Harlem. This Judaism was consistent with both Jewish tradition and American principles. This acculturated group did not want to be identified with the ghetto. (Gurock, p. 58) They wanted to break away from the economic and social bonds of the ghetto. They saw ghetto ideas as barriers to overcome in order to become part of American society. (Gurock, p. 86) They were modern thinking and had an elite leadership of East European businessmen, builders and real estate operators, who worked to expose all Jewish Harlemites to the values of America. However, they were troubled that Americanization was causing immigrants to become alienated from Judaism. They were afraid they would be converted by Christian missionary workers. These acculturated Jews responded by teaching that acculturation did not require the abandonment of their Jewish religious heritage. (Gurock, p. 58)

Some of the East European Jews did become more Americanized and they discovered a common identity with German Jews that they had not known earlier. (Rischin, p. 95) They changed their names from Greenbaum to Greene, Levy to Lamar. Their religious regimen relaxed with each passing week. Prayer diminished in regularity and duration. The prayer shawl and book was not used and men stopped wearing skull caps, untrimmed beards and side locks. They stopped wearing long black coats. (Rischin, p. 145) Religious festivals went limp along with the observance of the Sabbath. Purim and the Feast of the Maccabees went unnoticed. The Rabbis were not the honored magistrates and interpreters of the Law. They were ridiculed and said to be men that were good for nothing. They were unhonored and unknown. (Rischin, p. 148) These small-town Jews were shaped into a new people; they were transformed into modern Americans. Social and cultural institutions appeared to educate and inspire the immigrants into becoming Americans.

The East European acculturated Jewish leaders assisted the German Jewish community in establishing a settlement house called the Harlem Federation which taught that acculturation can be obtained with principles of good American citizenship and the moral principles of

Judaism. They also worked with German Jews through the modern Talmud torah system in institutions like the Uptown Talmud Torah, to separate the essence of traditional Judaism from its old-world shell. Therefore, Harlem began forming an Orthodox Judaism acceptable to those who wanted to become acculturated. Harlem became conducive to rapid Americanization while maintaining and even strengthening Jewish identification. In 1904 only a few institutions existed which were designed to fit Judaism to American culture. (Gurock, pp. 87, 88)

In 1904, Maurice'Harris led local synagogues in sponsoring Saturday afternoon services, as a step in reaching the Jewish youth. The Hebrew Educational Union of Harlem was created to bring Jewish religious training and a Jewish identification to children drawn from Harlem's German congregations. These services conformed to traditional Jewish dictates. Daniel P. Hays was president of the Hebrew Educational Union. Hays argued that a good Jew would make a good American citizen, showing the principles of Judaism were not a barrier to developing good American citizenship. (Gurock, p. 95) This notion allowed Jewish children to maintain their Jewish identity although the old traditional structure had been changed.

The East European elite founded in 1692 the Uptown Talmud Torah to serve the educational and religious needs of Russian Jewish children. Its first principal was Rabbi Joseph Sossnitz, a Russian Jew. The Uptown Talmud Torah received financial assistance from Reform

Jewish leaders Maurice Harris and Kaufmann Kohler of Temple Beth-El. (Gurock, p. 98) The Uptown Talmud Torah was slow in attracting children. It had a poorly trained Yiddish speaking faculty who taught only the alphabet, prayers and the Pentateuch and was incapable of reaching and influencing the American born generation. The Uptown Talmud Torah had a second principal, Rabbi Moses Reicherson, he died and was replaced by Zvi Malacovshy, a Russian immigrant who decided that a new type of organization was needed. The present system advocated separatism. The people supported the public school system and would not support any Jewish educational program. Zui Malacovsky designed a 3 level system for educating American-born students. They were taught Jewish history, morals and the achievements of the Jewish people, along with Hebrew words and phrases and basic religious concepts. Five percent of the students became interested in entering preministry instruction to prepare for leadership of the next generation of American Jews. (Gurock, p. 100) Malacovsky's plans were supported by most members of the Talmud Torah Association. He began raising funds to build a school. He appealed to the rich Jews in Harlem and received their allegiance and financial support. Another group of East European Jews worked to establish a Jewish-center uptown. It was called the Harlem Educational Institute, formed in 1904, for unacculturated Jews of Harlem. (Gurock, p. 101)

Within the Talmud Torah were people who did not

share modernization plans. (Gurock, p. 101) In 1905 leaders of the Talmud Torah Association and the Educational Institute pooled their assets and merged into a new Uptown Talmud Torah Association. It would become both a school that would teach Judaism and Hebrew as well as a social center in Harlem. In 1908 it had 1300 members that wanted to adhere to traditional dogmas; they organized opposition and were a frustration for the acculturated leader, David Cohen. (Gurock, p. 102) Cohen denounced those traditionalist members as reactionaries and blind. Philanthropist Jacob Schiff, an acculturated Jew, was asked by members of the Uptown Talmud Torah to assume a ten thousand dollar second mortgage on the newly constructed Harlem Hebrew Institute building. He said he would do it free of interest, only if the Jewish Theological Seminary and the Teachers' Institute, located in that building, would approve modern methods of instruction and modern ideas in all activities aimed at Americanizing the Jewish youth. (Gurock, p. 104) His demand was eventually accepted. The Uptown Talmud Torah's membership then increased and by 1911 there were 8,000 members using the institution's social, cultural and athletic facilities. When Cohen died his position was filled by a Jewish builder and philanthropist, Harry Fischel, an acculturated East European communal activist from Russia. He practiced the social gospel and wanted to develop the children's individual identities with the ethnic group to which they belonged. He built an Annex to give proper Jewish instruction along modern lines to children of the rich Jews on 115th Street, near Lenox Avenue. (Gurock,-p. 106)

Rabbi Schmarya Leib Hurwitz was the founder of Israel Salanter Talmud Torah who shared Fischel's dedication to blending Judaism with American ways. He also believed in the social gospel. He believed that the Uptown Talmud Torah was not adequately servicing many Jewish children and felt a need to have a Talmud torah near East 118th Street. He convinced the congregational directors to allocate classroom space within the synagogue building and opened it to the uptown children. (Gurock, p. 110)

The first attempt to establish a yeshiva was in 1907. Beth Hamidrash Ha-Gadol and Beth Knesset of Harlem organized and operated Yeshiva Rabbi Elijah Gaon M'Vilna in a public hall on Madison Avenue. Rabbi Moses Sterman of Suviak, Russia was hired as the Dean. He was given a mandate to create a school designed after the European model, to teach Gemara (a commentary on the Mishnah forming the 2nd part of the Torah) to American boys. (Gurock, p. 111) However, modern minded financial backers pressured Rabbi Sterman to instruct in English and insisted on allowing girls to enter the Yeshiva. They wanted an emphasis placed on biblical, Hebraic and general studies. This was unacceptable to the founders of Yeshiva Rabbi Elijah Gaon M'Vilna so Rabbi Sterman's group split and reestablished their own "European" Yeshiva, called Yeshiva Toras Hayim. The liberal faction of the Yeshiva Elijah

Gaon M'Vilna reconstituted itself as the Harlem Yeshiva. (Gurock, p. 111) The Harlem Yeshiva believed both that new Jewish leaders and teachers could only be trained in an intensive yeshiva program and that this next generation of leaders had to be rooted in both American values as well as Jewish tradition. In the Harlem Yeshiva students studied traditional texts half a day followed by general studies. These institutions along with others like it were the forerunners of contemporary modern yeshiva-Jewish day schools. (Gurock, p. 112)

The disputes and splits were shown above within the Yeshiva. Elijah Gaon M'Vilna signifies two separate sub communities in Harlem. Here it is seen that the ultra-Orthodox fought the non-Orthodox (new elite East Europeans) who argued that a Jewish identity could not survive using old-world values and institutions in America. The new elite believed that American educational methods must be applied to traditional studies. They wanted to perpetuate the essence of traditional Judaism. This was the American Orthodox point expressed in institutions like the Yeshiva University. The new American Orthodoxy standard was founded by spokesmen David Cohen and Harry Fischel. The European style Orthodox position was expressed by Yeshivas Toras Hayim in Harlem by a limited constituency. Its contemporary expression is found in Hasidic groups. (Gurock, pp. 112, 113)

Most acculturated parents avoided the cheder educational system. Others sent their children to Sunday

Hebrew school conducted in uptown congregations, or hired private tutors. Some thought Jewish religious education was unnecessary and did not train their children at all. (Gurock, p. 94)

German and East European activists worked together to establish communal institutions which taught a new understanding that Americanization did not require an end to one's Jewishness. They operated through the Harlem Federation. East Europeans placed their faith in a modernized traditional Judaism which spread though the American Talmud Torah. (Gurock, p. 94)

During the 1920's and 1930's second generation Jews who had grown up in American society and were educated in the public schools believed that they had no need for communal institutions dedicated to their entrance in American society. Many of these Jews saw no difference between themselves and other Americans. (Gurock, p. 115)

The Italian Americans religion, like the Jewish religion, was the focal point of the Italian community in East Harlem. In order to be accepted by Americans into the American culture, they, like the East European Jews, had to adapt to a religious tradition different than the one they traditionally practiced in Europe. The essay will show how the Italian tradition incorporated the individual into the collective Italian family and the larger community within East Harlem. In 1899 the Italian community was located in East Harlem on 3rd Avenue between 110th Street and 116th Street; Italians lived there along with Irish and

German Catholics. (Robert Anthony Orsi, The Madonna of 115th Street (New Haven: Yale University Press, 1985), p. 16) Jews moved into East Harlem at about the same time. (Orsi, p. 17) Harlem's residential population prior to 1900 were either native-born or of West European ancestry. Irish and German influence ended during the first decade of the 20th century when Italians, Russian Jews and Blacks made their incursions into Harlem. Between 1900 and 1910, the Irish and German population decreased in Harlem by approximately 50 percent. Italians were self-segregated in their enclave east of 3rd Avenue. By 1910, 59,200 Italians relocated to East Harlem, east of 3rd Avenue and south of 125th Street, except for an area from 99th Street to 104th Street between 1st and 3rd Avenues, where Jews dominated. Approximately 13,000 Italians lived elsewhere in Harlem. (Gurock, p. 50)

By 1920 Irish and Jewish populations began to leave East Harlem to the more pleasant areas of the South Bronx. At that point East Harlem was mainly Italian. Italian Harlem extended from 104th Street to 120th Street, between 3rd Avenue and the river. (Oris, p. 17) However, there was a mixture of other groups living in that area. To understand the ethnic and racial makeup of Harlem at that time it is important to note that Black incursion also occurred between 1900 and 1910. Harlem's Black neighborhood was established in the northern parts of Central and East Harlem after 1905. Harlem at that time had 22,000 Black residents and 2/3's lived in a neighborhood bordered by 133rd to 140th Streets, between Park and Lenox Avenues, with 50% of their population between 5th and Lenox Avenues until after World War I. Then they made a major incursion into the predominantly Jewish sections of Lower Central and East Harlem. (Gurock, p. 50) Italians represented 79.6 percent of the population. They lived with 34 other ethnic and racial groups. According to Leonard Covello, in 1938, Jews, Germans, Irish, Blacks and Puerto Ricans were living there also. (Orsi, p. 17) Predominately the Italians lived in East Harlem, the Jews were further west and the Germans lived mostly south of the Italians. (Andrew Rolle, The Italian Americans (Oklahoma: Oklahoma Press, 1980), p. 24)

In order to understand Italian Catholicism in East Harlem, it is important to understand the role of the domus in Italian culture with the role of the Madonna and the unsanctioned popular religion of the Italian immigrants. One must also study the role of the church and priest in Italy and how it influenced the Italians attitude toward the church and priests in East Harlem. It is important to comprehend the role of Italian women and the events surrounding the devotion of the Madonna of Mount Carmel on East 115th Street, including an explanation of how the feast affected them socially, morally and psychologically and how it integrated the people and their culture together with their dead ancestors, the saints and their children. The procession is another element of the feast that is also important to understand. It helped Italians to identity their communal position in the Italian community. The route of the procession also defined the boundaries of what was considered to be Italian Harlem. In addition it is important to understand the role of sacrificing and suffering and vows made to the Madonna and their domus', in order to understand the conflicts which their behavior created with the more modern non-Italian groups within the larger ethnically and racially mixed neighborhood of Harlem.

The domus played a central role in Italian East Harlem. The basic unit of the extended Italian family was the domus. The domus included the nuclear family along with grandparents, aunts, uncles and cousins to the fourth degree. It also included the physical property owned by the domus. In addition the domus contained nonblood members called comari and compari who were so closely associated with the domus that they received the same respect as any member of the domus proper. (Richard Gambino, Blood of My Blood (New York: Doubleday & Company, Inc., 1974), p. 19)

The domus judged a person's character; it determined whether a person was good or bad depending upon how much loyalty the person gave to the domus. (Rolle, p. 154) Loyalty to the domus was greater than the loyalty shown to the church or state. (Dinnerstein, p. 55) Though a member would not die for the church or state, he would die for a member of the domus. (Rolle, p. 154)

The domus provided the Italians with a meaning of

life and their moral guidelines. Individuals within the domus received their identity from their position in the domus. The domus was the foundation of Italian Harlem's culture. In 1912 an Italian American priest, Louis Giambastiani, tried to explain the Italian Catholic's religious sentiment to American Catholics. He said they are a religious people, but for many religion was within the walls of the home which, to them, is religious. (Orsi, p. 75) He went on to say that the Italian home and family, called the domus, is the religion of the Italian Americans. (Orsi, p. 77)

The immigrant's home was his sanctuary. His extended family was expected to be loyal. The family was ruled by the parents and what the father said was law. However, Italian men assigned a strange role to the women within their families. Men showed traits of aggression, but women assumed subordinate, nonerotic roles. Women were both worshiped and dominated, they spent their life waiting upon men, including their sons; women were both exalted and demeaned. (Rolle, p. 111) The male children were prevented from becoming independent. Mothers aligned their children against their father; he was alone and condemned. Outwardly he appeared to rule the family, but really the wife had that sickly power. She offered her entire being as a martyr for her children. (Rolle, p. 112)

The role of the Catholic Church was not as great as the role of the domus in the religion of the Italians. The family was the most critical institution for Italians and the

Catholic Church was second. (Orsi, p. xviii) The Catholic religion was only appreciated because it provided occasions like Christmas, Easter holidays or feast days when Italian Catholics could celebrate their devotions to their patron saints for the purpose of obtaining their favors. (Gambino, p. 201) The Italian Catholic peasant believed in God and the saints, but only went to church at critical periods of his life, on occasions of which he would be the participant, such as birth, marriage and death. Italians were faithful attendants at baptisms, weddings, and funerals and went to church on the days of their feast; they mainly attended at this time because these rites of passage celebrated the Italian Catholic's life and the lives of their families which was their religion. Only then did it make sense, according to their religious values, to go to church. (Gambino, p. 193)

The Italian tradition contained a mechanism, like the Jewish tradition mentioned earlier, which when employed had the effect of creating communities out of individuals. One of the central meanings of the annual festa was the power and authority of the domus *over* the lives of the individuals. (Orsi, p. 229) The identities of the individuals were tied to the larger identity of the domus, dominated by their mother, who protected them.(Orsi,p.177)

A former resident of East Harlem explained he was taught two things: religion and family life. The family, he was taught, provided everything. The domus, which they had in Italy, they created again in America. The adults taught their children to perpetuate it. It consisted of a strict family order, with disciple, family loyalty. and mutual support which was an expression not unlike the social gospel. (Orsi, p. 78) They all shared in the maintenance of the domus, although at times, they rebelled against its constraints. (Orsi, p. 79)

The Madonna was brought to East Harlem, by Italian immigrants from Italy, as a link to Italy and a reminder of their past. The Italians were separated from their homes, their families and their friends. The presence of the Madonna, on East 115th Street, made their separation easier to bear. (Orsi, p. 23)

The Church of Our Lady of Mount Carmel was built by the Italian immigrants themselves and the 1st mass was heard on Dec. 8, 1884. The funds to build the church mainly came from the German and Irish groups who lived there. (Orsi, p. 54) The church and the devotion had such importance in East Harlem that when people were asked to tell the story of their lives they told about the building of the church, which immigrants called "la casa della nostra mamma." (Orsi, p. 64)

When the Madonna came to the new world, she was relegated, along with the immigrants, to the basement of Our Lady of Mount Carmel to worship, despite the fact that 86 out of 90 children baptized there, in 1884, were Italian. (Orsi, p. 54) She was an embarrassment to the Catholic Church. The Madonna eventually was taken from the basement of Our Lady of Mount Carmel and installed on the main alter in 1927. (Amfitheatrof, p. 244) The Madonna was allowed to leave the basement when the Italians gained some control of political power. At this time, LaGuardia entered Congress and the Italian- language was accepted *by* the Board of Education as a subject to be taught in public schools. (Orsi, p. 50)

The Madonna was crowned on July 10, 1904, in front of many people in East Harlem on 115th Street, by the order of Pope Leo XIII. This ecclesiastical procedure elevated the shrine in the church to a sanctuary within the church of Our Lady of Mount Carmel on 115th Street. (Orsi, p. 61)

When Pope Leo XIII crowned the Madonna he accomplished two things. First, he asserted the triumph of Marian Catholicism over modernism. Second, he created a presence of a Rome-centered Catholicism in Italian East Harlem. (Orsi, p. 63) The crown symbolized papal power and showed the Italian people that the Vatican cared about them in their new home. (Orsi, pp. 63, 64)

The crown also became associated with the people themselves as it was their gold that made the crown. The gold was donated to the Madonna by the immigrants in gratitude for the graces they received from her. The immigrants sacrificed the gold from objects that were dear to them and had symbolic meaning. The objects they sacrificed were objects used by the people as they celebrated occasions associated with the "rites of passage". They gave their rings, brooches, and family heirlooms a great sacrifice made to the Madonna who was the center of their moral world. (Orsi, p. 64) The Madonna, in this manner, was petitioned by family members to protect the members of their domus.

The divine figures in the devotion were symbolic of people in a domus relationship. They were La mamma celest, called Mary, and Jesus her loving son, the brothers Cosmos and Damian. Saint Anthony was a popular "compari". (Orsi, p. 226)

The meaning of the devotion to the Madonna of 115th Street was shaped by the Italian people rooted in the history of their conflicts, struggles and expectations. The Madonna was the symbol of a Virgin, and a mother; she was at the center of a ritual, the focus of a drama to be acted out. (Orsi, p. 163) Their devotion to the Madonna was based on their devotion to their families and their Italian traditions. (Orsi, p. 168) Devotion to the symbol of the Madonna was devotion to a woman, a mother and a virgin. Because the Madonna represented women, she, while being honored, allowed Italian men to be symbolically faithful to the women they left in Italy. (Orsi, p. 164) She was the visible link between Italy and East Harlem. This belief may be due to the pagan belief that what looks alike, acts alike, influences alike and produces alike. Faithfulness expressed to women also meant faithfulness to the moral and cultural system of the domus (the extended family) which was signified and dominated by women. Being faithful to the Madonna meant being faithful to women and the values that the Italian people internalized. The house in which the Madonna lived, the church, was thought of as their mother's house in which they received security, peace, protection and pardon in this strange land. (Orsi, p. 165) The Madonna was healing their suffering, grief and anguish. She gave the Italian Catholics safety, relief and peace as they participated in the festa. (Gambino, p. 202)

As children express their needs to their mother, the Italian immigrants, mostly women, described their needs to the Madonna during the feast, calling out their troubles to her in the streets or in church, in the presence of their neighbors, and horrified American Catholics, Irish, German and others, who were embarrassed. (Donna R. Gabaccia, From Sicily to Elizabeth Street (Albany: University of New York Press, 1984), p. 9) The problems that these women presented were somewhat related. They contained a problem that was physical or psychological that threatened the domus. (Orsi, p. 227) Many of the problems that the women presented revealed a concern for the threats found in the urban environment. (Orsi, p. 174) Their pleas, as mothers, were for the domus of which they were the caretakers to the symbol of a powerful mother, the Madonna, who would intervene and heal a parent or a child, within the domus, thereby saving the domus. (Rolle, p. 157) The stories of healing brought attention to the vulnerability of the family along with the comfort that the domus would always triumph through the intervention of their mother, the Madonna. (Orsi, p. 177) Women seemed to doubt that a male God could understand them. They turned to a female divinity who suffered for her child, as they did. She was powerful and could understand women and their problems. The community knew the power and authority of women and they expected that the Madonna, being a woman, had the same power in the ordering of the divine. (Orsi, p. 227) Her assistance in resolving the problems that threatened the domus resulted in the reintegration of the domus and sanctified it. (Orsi, p. 177)

In primitive religion, a fetish can be a natural object or it can be manufactured. Its purpose is to bring good luck. It is worshiped and prayed to. The Madonna seemingly was attributed with those same characteristics. The statue had a likeness to a Mediterranean woman holding her small son. Mother and child had real hair. She had a woman's full figure with broad hips and ample bosom, a round face and delicate neck. Both mother and son were holding scapulars. The statue resembled those in Salerno, Naples, Avellino and other towns in southern Italy. (Orsi, p. 12) She wore a gown and was decorated with rings, watches, earrings and chains given to her by men and women who believed she helped them out of difficulty or pain. She was surrounded by canes, crutches and braces left there by people who the Madonna was believed to have healed. (Gambino, p. 196)

During the feast the Italian immigrants received scapulars from the church, the symbol of their mother's house, in return for sacrifices that they made during the feast. Scapulars of the Madonna were given out to protect the body and defend the soul. People carried the scapulars in their wallets and purses; they kept them in their bedrooms and kitchens for protection, a cure, consolation and comfort. Scapulars were ties that bound members of the community together, as well as the self with the domus and the divine. (Orsi, p. 173) The scapular was a kind of good luck charm which represented the superstition of their popular religion. (Gambino, p. 200) Superstition according to the official Catholic Church is forbidden. It credits power to divinities greater than God, who Catholicism views as omnipotent.

In summary, the Madonna was the source of the connection between the self and the community. The people acknowledged the centrality of the Madonna in shaping the community. (Orsi, p. 182) She was the communities' sacred mamma, she drew people out of each domus, interconnecting their social responsibility and reciprocity to each other, as they shared in each others pain. The ritual of the devotion affirmed the public role of the women of the domus, who shaped the social life of their respective domus', as the Madonna shaped the social life of Italian Harlem. (Gambino, p. 14)

In East Harlem Italian Catholics practiced religion differently from the Irish and German Catholics. Irish and German Catholics followed the literal dictates of the official Roman Catholic Church. (Dinnerstein, p. 56) To the

Italian immigrant the Catholic Church in America was almost like a new religion. The Italian immigrant's religion was peculiar to the Americans, including the Irish Catholics. It fed on devotions, pilgrimages, shrines and holy pictures. (Orsi, p. xv) The Italian Catholic's religion was a popular religion practiced in the streets and practiced by the people without the aid of priests. It consisted of activities outside the dictates of the organized church and, unlike the Irish Catholics, they had a peasant spirituality. Italian Catholics believed in magic and folk practices which were not condoned by the Irish priestly hierarchy of the official Roman Catholic Church. (Rolle, p. 156)   The Italian's religion was strewn with beliefs in the forces of good and evil and faith in magical practices. (Gambino, p. 214) At the heart of his religion was the feast--a social occasion for merrymaking and a religion for the masses. (Joseph Lopreato, Italian Americans (New York: Random House Inc., 1970), p. 89)

The role of women in popular religion can be understood within the Italian community of East Harlem by analyzing the drama surrounding the feast of the Madonna. The role of the Italian immigrant women is important to understand. Women were expected, in public, to show subservience to their husbands. (Gambino, p. 24) However in East Harlem when Protestants came to their door to reform them according to their standards of hygiene, it was the Italian mother who confronted them. (Orsi, p. 134)

In East Harlem Italian women were matriarchs, the sources of power and authority, hidden within their domus centered society. (Gambino, p. 14) Women decided who would be, or not be, members of the domus. (Gabbaccia, p. 4) They identified the comari who were to be respected by their husbands and children. They were the guardians of the traditional mores in Italian Harlem. They were treated with special respect and consulted on all family decisions. (Gambino, p. 213) Some were respected for their special knowledge in magic rituals; it was women who were able to heal ailments caused by curses. (Gambino, p. 199)

Women sacrificed, showed grief, and made many decisions for the well-being of their families. Women were expected to express the grief of their domus. It was their job to mourn the dead. (Orsi, p. 132) One of Covallo's students said his mother was self-sacrificing and a keystone to the family. (Orsi, p. 133) Mothers were the disciplinarians who meted out punishment instructing their husbands to administer it. They controlled who their children married. They evaluated them and decided if they would make a good addition to their domus. (Gambino, p. 7) When a member of the domus wanted something the mother was cajoled, entreated and manipulated, sometimes for weeks until it she gave maternal sanction. (Orsi, p. 134) It has been shown here that the role of the women within their domus' was similar to the role of the Madonna within the larger Italian community of East Harlem.

To understand the role the church and priests played

in the lives of Italian immigrants in East Harlem it is important to examine their traditional roles in Italy. Many Italians in Italy did not attend church services. (LoPreato, p. 87) According to the Catholic Church it made them bad American Catholics. However the Italian Catholic immigrants did not believe that it made them good or bad Catholics. (Orsi, p. xvii) The Churches in the agricultural villages of Italy were empty. Religious services were attended by a small number of old ladies, spinsters and old gentlemen wanting to establish their salvation before they died. Young and middle-aged males went to church only on special occasions; even then they would congregate outside the church and chat instead of attending the services inside. (Lopreato, p. 87) The non-church-going men would marry in a Roman Catholic ceremony to please their brides and families. (Rolle, p. 157). Italian men were not loyal to the church or state, they would not defend them with their lives as they would in order to protect their families. (Rolle, p. 154)

The religiosity of the southern Italians was undermined by their attitude toward the priest. They referred to the priests as parasites. The confessions that priests heard from their wives were considered to be an intrusion into their lives and a threat to their control over the family. (Rolle, p. 155) In some places the priest was the only educated person in the village. He was not compassionate and did not respect his parishioners; he was inclined to treat them with haughtiness. Peasants accused priests of wanting to sleep with their wives. (Lopreato, p. 88) The Catholic Church traditionally exploited the peasants in southern Italy where they owned 75 percent of the local land. The priest, in East Harlem, was a reflection of the cruel landlord that they knew in southern Italy. (Lopreato, p. 89)

The Italian religion was practiced not in church, but in the streets of East Harlem. Analyzing some central events in the feast show how this was true. Food played a central role in the Italian immigrant's street theology. Small vendors were everywhere selling food, beer and wine. The smells and the tastes reminded the Italians of Italy, making Harlem feel like home through association. Central to the feast was eating. (Gambino, p. 16) Eating was the sacrament of the home. Italians treated the Sunday meal as being more important than attendance at mass. Meals were cooked in the home by members of the domus. (Orsi, p. 4) The food was later eaten in the streets. Eating food in the streets became a symbol that sanctified the streets and integrated it with the home. (Orsi, p. 173) As the home was sacred, through eating, the streets became sacred. (Orsi, p. 4)

The role of the feast in Italy, as in East Harlem, and the devotions that were expressed there had the effect of socially integrating the people. The people often participated in a devotion to the saint of their hometown, this participation in a communal event was the affirmation of their belonging to a particular paese. (Gabbaccia, p. 61)

The feast symbolically integrated the individual's destiny with the destiny of his community. The church and devotion belonged to the entire community of East Harlem, not to any particular group of Italians from any particular region of Italy. (Orsi, p. 65) The Italian Catholic tradition of popular religion helped the Italian immigrants face the dirty and dangerous community of Italian Harlem. The people were able to use their religious solidarity, by transforming the devotion of the Madonna from the regional celebration in honor of the protectress of Polla, in Italy, to a celebration in honor of the Madonna at 115th Street. It gave all the people of East Harlem, from different towns, a community consciousness and solidarity. The church of Mount Carmel was identified with 115th Street and the Virgin was referred to as "the Madonna of 115th Street". Therefore, the Madonna was identified with the church and the street; this constituted a sacralization of Italian Harlem. The people considered 115th Street to be holy because the Madonna lived there. Therefore, the devotion to the Madonna was able to overcome the southern Italian regional identities, normally associated with the Madonna, and absorbed them into the church at 115th Street. (Orsi, p. 180) It was this tradition which Italian Catholics had to leave behind to become modernized. They had to leave their street theology and enter the official Catholic Church to become recognized as Americans. Catholic Church officials wanted the Italian Catholics to worship in the Church along with the

American Catholics.

To understand the Italian Catholic religion, which is the family itself, it is crucial to observe the feast. In watching the feast the people were both participants and audience of a drama, a drama that revealed their deepest values and perceptions. By participating in the drama they were better able to understand themselves. In observing the annual celebration of the Madonna the moral values and attitudes of the men and women of Italian Harlem, their perceptions of reality, and understandings of the good life, the good person, the bad person and the destiny of the people, can be understood. The celebration was an expression of the needs and values of the community. The devotion was a means of confirming and enforcing these perceptions and orientations. Within it, the hidden structures of power and authority were revealed. It was there that the people expressed their rage, assumptions and demands of their culture in a way that was approved and contained. In the feast the people purged themselves of the emotions in the domus-centered society and reinforced it. In their devotion to the Madonna they attempted to deal with tensions and crises that the immigrants faced in this strange land. (Orsi, p. xviii)

The feast was morally and psychologically a reintegration of the people into their culture. It was a time when people recalled their communal values, their consciousnesses and memories between their mother's house and the house of the Madonna. The older immigrants were able to live out in a sacral context the moral structure of their community and were able to introduce their children to that world. It educated all the generations in its moral values, it consoled them both physically and spiritually. It ratified the legitimate demands of the domus. It shaped the community of Harlem and linked it with their old home. The feast was an arena in which the struggles of the people would be expressed in the presence of the divine Mother. (Orsi, p. 218)

The feast celebrated and confirmed that the community's destiny was a shared destiny. It confirmed the communion of the people and their saints, the living and the dead, the people present and those that were absent. (Gambino, p. 205) The street theology proclaims that the divine and the human have a mutual responsibility to each other. It taught a general characteristic of primitive religion, not believed by some American Protestants, that humans must treat all things sacred with respect and caution because of their supernatural potency and that divine power are awesome and not always comprehensible. Divine power must be approached with love and fear. The Italian Catholic street theology taught that the living, the dead, the holy and the human, live together with the saints; that what God proposes, people must respect. The Catholic street theology taught that people should behave out of a collective, rather than an individual, mode and that their destiny is shared and suffering for the well-being of the family can become a triumph. By sacrificing, primitive religion teaches that a way is opened in a person for the supernatural power to enter himself and influence him. All this brought an ancient religious heritage to East Harlem. The American Catholics, downtown, were embarrassed by the Mediterranean spirituality in the streets. They were offended by the noise, food and emotion in the presence of the sacred. (Orsi, pp. 230, 231)

The feast did not end with the visit to the sanctuary. At night there were concerts, people danced in the streets until morning. Meats donated by butchers were raffled off (sacrificed) and residents prepared feasts for their visitors. The families and their neighbors visited and ate all night in celebration. (Orsi, p. 12)

The trip to attend the feast was a symbolic recapitulation of the immigrants' trip to the new land. (Orsi, p. 167) People traveled from all over the U.S. to attend the feast. Some walked, flew, or took boats crossing the water from Brooklyn, Staten Island, New Jersey, or California etc. This journey ended at their Madonna's feet in East Harlem. (Orsi, p. 165) People arrived in Harlem from all over the United States. They came to stay in any accommodations that they could find. Some stayed with the compari or relatives for up to four or five days, sometimes up to two weeks. The Italians of East Harlem prepared for the visit, cleaning, cooking and scrubbing clean their buildings, sidewalks and streets. (Orsi, p. 1) This enabled the extended family of the Italians to come together. Cousins met cousins from all over the United

States. People stayed up all night, talking, eating and attending confession, to prepare themselves for asking the Madonna to intervene in their lives which would protect the well-being of their families. (Orsi, p. 2) The feast depicted a great homing, men and women drawn back to Harlem by the power of the Madonna. The Madonna and other saints, like the immigrants had immigrated to the new world with their people. She provided continuity between the old world and the new. Her graces were given to the people, in East Harlem, thereby sanctifying their decision to leave Italy for the new world. (Orsi, p. 167)

On July 16, each year, on the feast day, the people would walk to the church in their finest clothes to pay proper respect to the Virgin. The people decorated their buildings with crepe, flags, colored lights and blankets which hung from their windows. Around the church were games of chance, vendors of religious articles; booths filled with wax replicas of internal human organs, limbs and heads which were used to represent someone who had been healed by the Madonna. (This was evidence that the Italian Catholics believed in "imitative" magic, a subdivision of magic that assumes that things that look alike, act alike and therefore, influence and produce a like effect) These were sold along with holy cards, statues of Jesus, Mary and saints. (Orsi, p. 3) There were also big heavy candles sold which were bought by the faithful to be carried as a burden through the blistering heat of the procession. The weights of the candles corresponded with the seriousness of the grace that the devout were asking of the Madonna. (Gambino, p. 208) Some candles weighted as much as the person for whom prayers and sacrifices were being offered. (Orsi, p. 3) If it was too heavy for one person to carry the burden it was shared by other members of the domus. (Orsi, p.-4)

Candles represented a family crisis. Individuals during the procession submitted to carrying huge burdensome candles. Carrying them in the heat caused them to suffer. They were begging the Madonna to heal their pain and thanking her for their safe keeping, while they were acknowledging the power of the domus over them. (Amfitheatrof, p. 243) The people who carried the candle were sharing the responsibility for carrying the symbol of their domus' crisis publicly through the streets, in full view of their neighbors and the Madonna; they were acknowledging their responsibilities in the domus and literally bowing down to its authority.   (Orsi, p. 178)

The Procession of the Madonna through the streets played a role in Italian Harlem. The manner in which the procession was ordered told everyone where their place was in the larger community. It helped raise their esteem and shape their identity. In the afternoon, members of the neighborhood societies went to the church to take their places in the procession. They were dressed in their best suits or rented tuxedos. They would pull the float through the streets of East Harlem; a task that was an honor and a privilege. At the head of the procession was East Harlem's elite, including judges, lawyers, doctors, politicians and funeral directors. Merchants and the entire grammar school marched in the procession. The Band played Italian music. Behind the societies was the statue of the Madonna mounted on a float decorated with flowers and white ribbons. Little girls clothed in white surrounded the Madonna. With a signal from the priest the music began to play, the fireworks exploded and the procession began. (Orsi, p. 6)

The procession through the streets had two great functions, first it made the Madonna physically accessible to the people so they could interact with her and the larger community. Second, the procession marched along the boundaries of Italian Harlem identifying those boundaries and sanctifying them. Being accessible to the people she became the focal point for sacrifice and suffering from which the devoted could obtain divine favors. The streets were filled with the devout on sidewalks and in windows. Women chanted, they walked behind the Madonna and were segregated from the men. The surviving family members fulfilled the vows of their mothers and relatives who were now dead. Individuals honored the vows of their respective domus', whether they were made by themselves or dead relatives, whom they respected, honoring those vows that the dead made in the past for the sake of their domus'. This practice revealed that the power of the domus was greater than the individual's power. (Orsi, p. 7) The children thereby shared the burden of pain in fulfilling these vows. (Orsi, p. 170) Another way in which the Italians honored their dead ancestors was by putting their pictures of the dead alongside the statues of saints in their homes. Also, they visited the cemetery to show their continuing respect and love. There was an intimate communion between the living and the dead. (Orsi, p. 229) In primitive religion the ancestral spirits want to take care of the descendents but will only do so if the living pays them proper respect. It is therefore customary to make offerings at the grave to placate the dead. (John B. Noss and David S. Noss, Man's Religions (New York: Macmillian Publishing Company, 1984), p. 19) In this manner the dead were not forgotten and included in the feast of the living.

Women threw themselves at the base of the Madonna, to beg for help for their families. Before the community a mother would publicly identify her family's needs to the Madonna in detail. They pinned their contributions of dollars and jewelry (sacrifices for bribery) to the vestments of the Madonna which later would be used to beautify the church. (Amfitheatrof, p. 243) Penitents walked barefoot on the searing pavement. Women bore heavy candles. They wore Franciscan-style robes during the procession and some promised to wear them for months, or even a year as a serious vow. (Orsi, p. 8) They bore the pain to repay the graces they received from the Madonna. (Orsi, p. 10)

They brought their children with them to the devotion and they shared their tradition with their children. (Orsi, p. 169) Children helped support the old who were marching. One emphasis of the procession was to transmit to their children their deep faithfulness to their tradition. (Orsi, p. 170) Therefore, what took place at the feast were the integration of young people into traditional values, and the communal reaffirmation of those values, between the individual, the family and the community. (Orsi, p. 172) It was in the procession that the parents and children fulfilled vows of their domus together to the Madonna. (Orsi, p. 170)

The people shared with their neighbors and their extended family, including their comari, each others' lives during the festa. (Orsi, p. 171) They were in the presence of their "mamma" of the old world where they had learned from their mothers what reality was, what was good and bad, what their values were and the values of their community.

In the procession the Italians could recall the traditional religious processions of southern Italy. They could recall the little shrines to Mary all over Italy. Once a year they could reestablish their memories and relocated their stability by returning there in religious spirit.

The procession went down every block marking out the "Italian quarter" of Harlem. The Madonna reshaped east Harlem as an Italian colony. The feast was a declaration of the presence of Italians in East Harlem to the

Irish and German Catholics, who were embarrassed by them, and some American Protestants who felt threatened by them. (Rolle, p. 156) This procession intimidated non-Italians who understood that this was an expression of local Italian prominence and that they were not welcome to join the procession. (Orsi, p. 163) This also claimed the streets for the people; the Madonna claimed them by blessing them and people claimed them by keeping them clean. The streets were an extension of the home in Italy. The Madonna in the streets was a moral authority over the gutters which helped to incorporate the streets into the domus-centered society. (Orsi, p. 164)

The children of the Italian immigrants, unlike their parents, preferred to celebrate in a church building, in a serious and dignified manner, not on the streets. They felt shame seeing their parents tramping over hot street pavement obstructing traffic while carrying the statue of the favorite saint in a procession. The children would rather support the church using a monthly collection than pin a dollar bill to a ribbon suspended from the saint's neck. (Orsi, p. xvi)

Individuals suffered on behalf of the domus by making a sacrifice to the Madonna. In their prayers and promises made to the Madonna on the day of the festa, the people transformed their suffering into sacrifice and triumphed over it. The sacrifice provided for triumph over a problem which a family member suffered. Religious sacrifice is something that is freely chosen. It is a suffering that is freely assumed. In the devotion people were able to suffer by doing penitential practices. (Orsi, p. 203) The vows that the Italian women made to the Madonna were a crude form of bartering with the divine or an attempt to bribe their destiny. It was a type of contract. Some people even kept a check list of the payments they made to divine figures. They had a client relationship. The people sacrificed by suffering to gain the attention of the divine to get special favors. (Orsi, pp. 220, 221) Those devoted had to show a stoic fortitude in the face of adversity. They expected a reciprocal relationship with the saints or the Madonna and were angry if proper respect was not returned to them for their sacrifices. The saints were expected to be faithful upholding the standards of the domus. They often expressed anger against them if the saints did not respond favorably. (Orsi, p. 224) It seemed pathological in its origins and consequences. The people seemed to want to bind themselves to the divine by creating sympathy through a covenant based on pain. (Orsi, pp. 220, 221) Paying homage to her, (another ritualistic characteristic) glorifying her and beseeching her to reward them with favors usually related to securing the needs of their domus. The vow was made to the Madonna. It involved voluntary suffering on the part of the person making the vow, for the purpose of trading one's chosen pain to replace an unbidden pain. They walked barefoot through the streets of Italian Harlem. This religious sacrifice allowed the people to believe that they had control over their destinies in a world where they would otherwise feel bound by severe social and economic constraints. They freely assumed suffering as opposed to merely enduring pain; this religious experience gave them relative freedom in their lives which otherwise were ruled by necessity. (Orsi, p. 203) Also, when a family member knew that someone was suffering on his behalf it created a bond between the two members of the family. It made rebellion against that family very difficult. Therefore, the source of comfort was also the source of entrapment. (Orsi, p. 204)

To understand why sacrifice and suffering should lead to a favor deserved, it is important to understand the Italian Catholics notion of the significance of blood. Blood bound the members of the domus together; they were related by having the same blood. The blood on the face of the crucified Jesus was seen as the covenant between the divine and the domus. The Italian people, who knew the meaning of blood bonds, understood that the bleeding God established an intimacy between the people and the divine. They believed, because blood was the basis of bonding between the individual members of the family and the domus that they, through bleeding in sacrifice, could expect reciprocal respect from the bleeding divine, (Orsi, p. 225)

The sacrificial suffering through the vows made to the Madonna was a demonstration of respect for the Madonna. (Orsi, p. 223) However, this was a respect not only of love, but of fear. Sacrifice, to the Madonna for the well-being of the domus, was also a discipline. Through suffering people learned patience. The person who suffered for the well-being of the domus was judged by the community to be a good person. (Orsi, p. 224) The people were showing her, and their domus, what they were willing to do for her, and their domus. Their suffering was a gesture of gratitude for the Madonna's care. (Orsi, p. 223) The Italian people of East Harlem acknowledged their dependence on the divine and expressed their fear of it and gratitude for it. The vows were signs of their love, devotion and faith. (Orsi, p. 229)

The Italian immigrants brought holy figures into their homes and performed rituals of respect toward them and included them in the life of the domus. (Gambino, p. 201) When the Madonna was carried back on the altar she was surrounded by hundreds of candles and wax body parts. The people came to the sanctuary to be healed. They prayed, (a primitive religious characteristic used to influence spiritual powers to coerce or force spirits to yield) wept and spoke incomprehensible words. Some laughed in uncontrollable gratitude for a grace they had received from the Madonna. It was customary for a woman who had a child that was healed by the Madonna to bring that child to the feast dressed in the best clothes she could afford and, at the altar, offer those new clothes to be distributed to the poor of the parish. (Orsi, p. 11) This gesture was in keeping with the notion of the social gospel. Therefore, the sacred world was not only in the churches but also in the family through hospitality and friendship. (Orsi, p. 226)

To understand the conflict between the Italian ritualists and the Protestants it is important to understand the American nativists. The descendants of the Puritan settlers saw a threat in the mass influx of new immigrants. Some were Germans who were viewed as having Marxist ideas. There were socialistic Scandinavians, bearded poles and Russians and Irish Catholics. Fear of Catholics was rooted in the American past. During the 16th and 17th centuries the English colonist attributed their victory to a Protestant democracy over the aristocratic feudal Catholic empire ruled from Paris by the Pope. Their presence in America revived their old fears. (Amfitheatrof, p. 103)

In addition to the Protestant nativist, the puritanical Irish hierarchy, in the Catholic Church in America and East Harlem accused the Italians of not being good Catholics. The immigrants appeared to be poor, ignorant and superstitious. (Amfitheatrof, p. 103) It was caused by Italy's three thousand-year-old traditions of magic, ritual and superstitious belief in deities which flowed into Christianity when it became the religion of Rome. They enjoyed pagan religious feasts. The Italians from the southern portion of the peninsula were the most fantastic and extravagant. (Amfitheatrof, pp. 242, 243)

When people perceive that their values and interests are being threatened they grow hostile and that hostility can be expressed by the threatened, by isolating themselves or trying to change the offensive group to adapt to or adopt their beliefs and notions. The Protestant denominations made an effort to wean Italians away from Catholicism to make them more Americanized. They were afraid that the Italians and East European Jews were penetrating America with their continental ideas of the Sabbath, along with a socialist's ideas of government, the communist ideas of property and the pagan's idea of religion. Few conversions were made among the Italians because the Catholic Church was too large a part of their tradition and could not be easily shed. (Amfitheatrof, p. 243) America's Protestant denominations converted only a fraction of the Italian population. Evangelization did not overcome the baffling religious practices and beliefs of the southern Italian peasants, a religion including superstitions, pagan rites and medieval rituals. It was the entrenchment of primitive tradition that helped the Italian immigrants to fend off Protestantism. (Rolle, p. 157) It is important to point out that Catholicism, as officially taught by the church, does not condone the Italian Catholic's popular devotions, such as the Madonna of 115th Street or the Madonna of Lourdes, Padre Pio, and the Shroud of Turin, etc. Theologians, when discussing the nature of Catholicism, do not even mention them. Earlier, the immigrants had to worship their Madonna in the lower church. This was because the leaders of the American church frowned on their devotion, considering it a public display of a Catholicism that was pagan and primitive. (Gambino, p. 195)

Ritualists, such as the Italian Catholics and

Orthodox Jews, were viewed by pietistic groups, which include the Methodists, to be an intrusion upon their traditional beliefs and ways of life. Pietists identified immigrants with crime, corruption and decay. They perceived that the immigrants threatened their culture and community. They did not want the immigrants to influence the government to implement their foreign standards over their American standards. (John Bodnar, The Transplanted (Bloomington: Indiana University Press, 1985), pp.198, 199)

When an ethnic community grows competitive tensions increase. Conflicts arise when one group feels that the other group possesses a real or perceived threat to its present or future interests or values in society. (Ronald H. Bayor, Neighbors in Conflict (Chicago: University of Illinois Press, 1988), p. 2) There was hostility between the different ethnic groups. Irish gangs attacked Jewish immigrants. The Irish also attacked Italians because they were sometimes used as strike breakers; they also held Italians responsible for the "imprisonment" of the pope by the forces of the Italian revolution. (Orsi, p. 17)

Catholicism was a source of conflict. The Protestants were concerned that their dominance in the country would be lost. They saw the Catholics as a papal conspiracy to rule America. Protestants viewed Catholicism as incompatible with American Ideals. (Bayor, p. 2) The Jews and Italians who were ritualists were striving to obtain power; they represented a vastly different value system than that practiced by the American Protestants. (Bayor, p. 3) Few problems existed between Italians and Jews. (Bayor, p. 4)

The Irish did not consider Italians to be good Catholics, but as intruders; this Irish attitude was reveled in an 1887 editorial in the New York Catholic Review which noted the disdain the Irish had for the Italian Catholics. (Bayor, p. 4)

The New York archdiocese under Archbishop Corrigna and then under Cardinal Farley, was ambivalent in its policies toward Italian popular devotion. On one hand they did not want to condone the feast because it would delay Italian assimilation. On the other hand they did not want to stop it because it would alienate the Italians who might turn away from the church and play into the hands of the Protestants. (Orsi, p. 56) The Irish clergy saw the devotion as pagan superstition and as sacrilegious. Although they were an embarrassment to American Catholicism, the clergy knew that the Italian people would not make contributions to the church or building a school. However, they would contribute extravagantly to the feast. Therefore, the clergy was, in part, financially dependent on the feast day of the Madonna. (Orsi, p. 57)

Bishop-Michael Corrigna of New York complained that Italian immigrants did not frequent the church and they made no offering to maintain the parish. Therefore, they should not be permitted to have their own parish. (Orsi, p. 61)

The Irish Catholics criticized the Italian Catholics,

because the Irish practiced religion differently. The Italian's Catholicism was based on paganism and less literally taken, whereas, the Irish Catholics interpreted the scriptures and Catholic theology. (Rolle, p. 159) American nativist saw Italian Catholicism as menacing and subversive, steeped in superstition and ignorance. (Rolle, p. 157) Related to superstition is trying to obtain an abnormal effect beyond the powers of nature by invoking a creature as though that creature were divine. Varieties are divination, magic, sorcery, and Satanism. (John A. Hardon S.J., The Catholic Catechism (New York: Doubleday and Company, 1975), p. 300) Americans thought that the southern Italians were violent. They said they were always carrying a stiletto or a revolver; they accused them as being quarrelsome, feuding and murderous. (Rolle, p. 66) Americans, in their arrogance, did not bother to understand the religion of their new neighbors, which the Irish called paganism. (Lopreato, p. 90)

The Irish and German Catholics thought that the Italian Catholics behaved in peculiar ways. They observed them gesturing, posturing, genuflecting, and praying in a special and specific manner which was rooted in the culture of the Italian people; (Orsi, p. xiii) some of which were not condoned by the official Catholic church which was under the influence of an Irish priestly hierarchy. (Amfitheatrof, p. 244) Irish Catholics could not understand Italian popular spirituality. "The Catholic World" published in 1888 a quote from Reverend Bernard Lynch who said that the spiritual condition of the Italian immigrants fed on pilgrimages, shrines, holy cards and devotions but lacked any understanding of the great truths of religion. (Orsi, p. 55)

The religion of the Italian Catholics was understood in a concrete down to earth way. It contained the sum of their values, ethnical convictions and the order of their reality. It was not a reality beyond their lives. It was something that they could experience. Religion to them was doing "what matters" in life and what mattered was loyalty to the domus. Traditionally, the church only provided the sacred rituals, practices, symbols, prayers used by the Italian people. (Orsi, pp. xvii, xviii)

As Catholicism was a threat to Protestantism so Protestantism was a threat to Catholicism. Protestants were accused by American Catholics as being idolaters of men. They believed in things that were only of the natural world, not the supernatural world. The natural world pertains to the worldly or temporal in contrast to the supernatural world of the Catholic ritualist which pertains to the spiritual or eternal world. (Harman, p. 302) Belief in the supernatural separates Catholics and Protestants. Prior to the emergence of spiritualism the Protestants did away with basic elements in Roman Catholicism's supernaturalist beliefs namely: transubstantiation, relics, and indulgences. (J. Gordon Melton, Encyclopedic Handbook of Cults in America (New York: Garland Publishing Inc., 1986), p. 61)

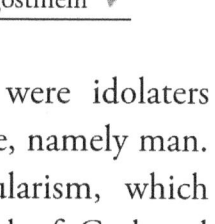

Catholics believed that Protestants were idolaters because they gave divine honors to a creature, namely man. Idolatry is almost synonymous with secularism, which substitutes idols of its own creation instead of God and worships them instead. Some Protestants believed that man was the master of his own destiny. They gave man the freedom to be an end unto himself, the creator of his own history. It was modern technical progress that nourished this idolatrous theory of self-sufficiency. (Hardon, p. 302)

The Irish believed the feast was wasteful and violent. An Irish policeman standing by and watching the festa said to Antonio Mangano, an Italian Protestant clergyman, that the money the Italians spent on their violent festival would be better spent building churches and orphanages. (Orsi, p. 55)

Italian Catholics criticized the Irish variety of Catholicism. They felt that the Irish priests and churches were cold with a puritanical strain. (Rolle, p. 156) Italians complained that Americans were disrespectful. They called Italians humiliating names including "ignorant dago, dirty wop, and greaseball" (Rolle, p. 51) The Italian Catholic could not understand the sight of grown Irish men taking communion on Sunday; counting rosary beads was shocking to the Italian man who was accustomed to thinking that religion was for women and children only. The Irish, unlike the Italians, mixed politics with religion. (Lopreato, p. 90)

Italians were offensive to the richer people who lived

nearby. They complained that their tenements smelled. (Osofsky, p. 82) The Americans ridiculed Italian Catholics for speaking broken English, talking loudly and gesturing with their hands. (Rolle, p. 51) On religious holidays and feast days, Italians were seen as doing strange things. Marionette shows or men grinding street organs could be seen everyday. Pushcarts and peddlers hawking their wares upset the peaceful neighborhood. (Osofsky, p. 82)

People from New York's better neighborhoods were horrified by the spectacle, of the feast, as they watched the lower classes at play. (Orsi, p. 4) German Catholics who had dominated Harlem in the early days, and others had come to watch. The working class Jews from East Harlem and the wealthy Jews and working class Blacks of West Harlem also came to watch; others came to pray at the shrine, while Irish policemen kept the peace. (Orsi, p. 6)

The Blacks were a major racial group living in East Harlem at the turn of the century. Many Blacks practiced a form of Protestantism. It will be shown that most American born Blacks were Methodist and Baptists while immigrant Blacks were mostly Episcopalian and Catholic. Many belonged to ritualistic groups of the occult, especially those from the West Indies. The Blacks were another religious group in Harlem whose religion was the focal point within their community. It was through the Black religious institutions that both the social gospel was practiced and the individual received his identity within the larger Black community of Harlem. Religion in this manner played the same role as it did for the Jews and Italians explained earlier.

The first Blacks to live in Harlem were slaves. The original wagon road constructed between New Amsterdam and Harlem was built by the Dutch West India Company's Negroes. (Gilbert Osofsky, Harlem: <u>The Making of a Ghetto. 1890-1939 </u>(New York: Harper & Row, Publishers, Inc., 1966), p. 83) Black squatters had settled in Harlem in the 1840's and 1850's along with the Irish immigrants.

In order to understand the organizations which were responsible for the development of Black Harlem it is important to understand the role of the Black churches and preachers, starting with the early churches. Blacks joined the Methodist Church in pre-revolutionary times, the congregations were separated and presided over by white preachers. In some churches the Blacks participated in the services although they were segregated. There were separate seats for whites and Blacks. Communion was given to the white members first; the Blacks were given communion second. (Harry A. Ploski, <u>The Negro Almanac African</u> American (New York: Gale Research Inc., 1989), p. 1306)

In the North in 1785, several influential Black members established their own places of worship. (Ploski, p. 1306) The Black Methodist church was founded in the early 1800's by Richard Allen, a former slave. (Martin E. Marty, <u>Christian Churches in the United States (New</u> York: Harper & Row, Publishers, Inc, 1987), p. 75) Blacks established their own churches because leaders believed that the race could be only be elevated from within the Black community by exhibiting race initiative, race pride, self-support, and participation in all duties and privileges of citizenship. In a church of their own the Blacks would be completely responsible for their own programs. The newly freed men and their children would have importance in the church and have an opportunity to develop self-reliance, which would quickly have the affect of uplifting the Black race. (August Meier, Negro Thought in America, 1680-1915 (Ann Arbor: The University Press, 1969), p. 131) It was ideals such as these that associated Blacks with the Puritans who were the model Americans that Blacks had to emulate. There were two large Black Methodist national groups that existed in Harlem: The African Methodist Episcopal Church and the African Methodist Episcopal Zion Church. (Marty, p. 75) The clergymen of both the A.M.E., A.M.E. Zion and Baptist churches believed that churches ran by Negroes were good for the Black community. (Meier, p. 131)

The Black community gradually increased in size in the late 19th century. Then, by 1899, 50,000 foreign-born Blacks from Cuba, the Virgin Islands, West Indies, Philippines and West Africa moved into Harlem. (Halliburton, p. 31)

In 1916, the boll weevil in the south caused cotton crops to be ruined, destroying the south's major industry. Jobs were drastically reduced. Blacks were laid off and moved north. World War I caused a labor shortage. The United States Department of Labor encouraged northern migration of Blacks. Some Blacks were recruited by private businesses to move north. (Halliburton, p. 30) Between 1914 and 1917, more than 400,000 southern Blacks moved north with almost 70,000 arriving in Harlem. (Halliburton, p. 31)

Black congregations were different from white dominated groups. Baptist and Methodist worship was evangelistic in tone and relied on the dynamism and personality of the preacher, rather than on strict adherence to the articles of faith. (Ploski, p. 1309) In Black churches, the congregation gave verbal feedback during the sermons. They sang Black hymns in which the congregation was free to improvise. The preachers offered hope, instead of warning of damnation. They avoided dwelling on the sins of the congregation. Black churches grew in Harlem because they served the needs of their congregations, both spiritually and socially. (Ploski, p. 1306)

The success of the real estate brokers John M. Royall, John E. Nail, Philip A Payton, Jr, and Henry Parker opened the way for Blacks to move into Harlem between 1911 and 1922. Black churches bought white church buildings or built new ones in Harlem. (Halliburton, p. 29)

Practically every major Black institution moved from downtown to Harlem by the early 1920's. White churches in Harlem were sold to Black churches. Germans, German-Jews, Irish, and others sadly moved away. Exclusive white denominations left East Harlem and sold their property to Black Baptists, Methodists and others. (Osofsky, p. 114) The most famous was the Collegiate Reformed Church (Second Dutch Reformed Church), founded in 1660; in 1930, it became the Negro Ephesus Seventh Day Adventist Church. (Osofsky, p. 121)

Evidence that the Black church depended on the Black congregation can be seen when studying their movement with the migration of the Blacks from downtown Manhattan to Harlem. The establishment of the church also shaped the Black community. In the early nineteenth century Blacks lived in the Five Points district, on the site of the present City Hall. (Osofsky, p. 9) Religious institutions of the district of Five Points included the Abyssinian Baptist Church, founded in 1808, located on present-day Worth Street. (Osofsky, p. 10) By 1900 the majority of religious institutions formerly established in Greenwich Village had move to the Tenderloin and San Juan Hill. (Osofsky, p. 14) The Tenderloin and San Juan Hill were populated in the 1890's by Blacks. The Tenderloin's boundaries were nowhere clearly defined. However, people considered the area to be between Twentieth Street and Fifty-Third Street. San Juan Hill stretched from Sixtieth to Sixty-fourth Streets, Tenth and Eleventh Avenues. (Osofsky, p. 12)   Stranded churches downtown were forced to follow their members to Harlem. In 1930, 90 million dollars were invested in churches. (Ottley p. 290)

Many Black churches realized large profits by selling property in the midtown area of Manhattan at high prices. Land value, uptown, in Harlem, had depreciated in value before WW I. (Osofsky, p. 15) They could afford the expense because they sold their property in the high priced downtown area and purchased land and property uptown which had gone down in value. (Halliburton, p. 29) The wealthier congregations not only built new churches in Harlem, but invested in local real estate, including in areas with restrictive covenants. Blacks were then permitted to live in buildings from which they had been denied entry. The churches became the largest Black property owners in Harlem. By becoming land holders, Black churches helped transform Harlem into a Black section. (Osofsky, p. 115) In this period, between 1911 and 1922, almost all the major Black churches moved to Harlem along with the social clubs and the Black Y.M.C.A. and Y.W.C.A. They changed Harlem into a   Black community. (Halliburton, p. 29)

In 1911, Harlem was not all Black. Blacks lived in a small section of Harlem on various blocks between 130th Street and 140th Street and between 5th and 6th Avenues. By 1914 Blacks lived in 1,100 houses within a 23 block area of Harlem. The Black population according to a National Urban League survey was 50,000. (Halliburton, p. 29) The area east of 5th Avenue down to 110th Street was called East Harlem and was occupied mostly by Italian and Jewish immigrants. (Jervis Anderson, This Was

Harlem (New York: Farrar Straus Giroux, 1982), pg. 62)

White residents became alarmed that Blacks were moving into the neighborhood. Black tenants were evicted. An Afro-American Realty company formed; it countered the white trend by leasing houses to Black tenants. Soon, Philip A. Payton and J.C. Thomas, both prosperous realtors, bought two 5 story apartment houses and dispossessed the whites and rented them to Blacks. St. Philips Protestant Episcopal Church bought a row of 13 apartment houses on 135th Street, between Lenox and 7th Avenues, costing $620,000 and rented them to Blacks. (Ottley, p. 185)

Strivers' Row is two blocks long on 138 and 139 Streets. It has an elegant row of houses. There are 158 four-story buildings commissioned in 1891 by builder David H. King and designed by leading architects of the day. The first occupants were millionaires like Randolph Hearst. In the 1920's the houses became inhabited by affluent Blacks such as doctors, lawyers, entertainers and educators. (Bruce Kellner, ed. The Harlem Renaissance (Connecticut: Greenwood Press, Inc., 1984), p. 13)

The Harlem slum of the twenties was the product of a deluge of Black migration to New York City. According to Reverend Dr. Powell, Harlem became the symbol of liberty and the Promised Land to Blacks everywhere. Many came from the south, especially Virginia and the Carolinas; others came from Georgia and Florida, formerly under-represented in earlier years. Also in this period many foreign born Blacks came into the area. (Osofsky, p. 128) As whites moved out of Manhattan, Blacks moved in. In Harlem between 1920 and 1930, 118,792 white people left the neighborhood and 87,417 Blacks arrived. Italian and Jewish immigrants had lived there. Now their children found the conditions of life in East Harlem to be unsatisfactory and they moved to newer areas. The Blacks moved into the flats vacated by Italians and Jews. By 1930, 164,566 Blacks, about 72 % of Manhattan's Black population, lived in Harlem. (Osofsky, p. 130)   Blacks were not permitted to live everywhere. Most Blacks were "jammed together" in Harlem, even those who could afford to live elsewhere, due to racial attitudes of segregation. (Osofsky, p. 131)   By 1930, most of Harlem's white population had fled and Blacks inhabited virtually the entire district. (Anderson, p. 59)

When the migration of Negroes from the south increased, white churches that formerly allowed small numbers of Blacks to participate in their regular services, now wanted them to get a place of worship of their own. (Osofsky, p. 41) New churches were developed in Harlem between 1870 and 1894. The Calvary Methodist Episcopal Church in 1883 had 40 members; ten years later the congregation was worshiping in a Gothic structure and two other missions were planned. (Osofsky, p. 79) Also founded were Presbyterian churches.

Harlem had a First German Baptist Church, a Temple of Israel of Harlem, St. Charles Borromeo Roman

Catholic Church and the Harlem Catholic Club. (Osofsky, p. 80)

Black churches played an important role in the development of Harlem, more than other institutions in the Black community. The church was the most stable and wealthy institution. As the Black population increased in the early 20th century so did the influence and wealth of the church. Membership trebled. Missions which began in storefronts or homes became independent and either bought or built new churches. (Osofsky p. 114),

Black Ministers preached in inadequate quarters in East Harlem. Mass services were sometimes held in "gospel tents", "mammoth tents, pitched on Harlem's empty lots." Downtown churches, prior to moving uptown, into Harlem, established Sunday schools and Bible classes in public halls and theatres. There, some congregations were so large that ministers had to hold 5 or 6 services each Sunday. (Osofsky, p. 114)

Mercy Street Baptist Church is an example of a church organized in Harlem by seven Blacks at the turn of the century. The congregation, at that time, met in a house owned by the Baptist City Mission. Later, the population grew and, by 1907, the Metropolitan Baptist (its new name),had 800 members and moved into a new building. Continued growth of the population made these facilities inadequate so they bought a white Presbyterian church in 1918. It became known as the Metropolitan Baptist and has remained there ever since. (Osofsky, p. 114)

In the Black ghetto the church was a major institution about which life revolved. The church helped organize the people of Harlem and worked for the improvement of conditions in the community. (Halliburton, p. 5) The Black church was one of the institutions that embraced a racial philosophy of self-help, solidarity, mutual support through fraternity, and economic progress as the keys to citizenship rights. (Meier, p. 219) The church had to meet the needs of its members. The church administered to religious needs and served as a social center, supplied relief to orphans and the aged, it promoted educational and cultural activities. (Kenneth B. Clark, <u>Dark Ghetto</u> (New York: Harper & Row Publishers, 1965), p. 92)

A good example of a major Black church was the Abyssinian Baptist Church which conducted a Vacation Training School, and the Union Baptist Church which operated an industrial school. (Clark, p. 92) A few churches opened summer camps outside the city for Black youths. In the church the Black could attend concerts, lectures, discussions, reading rooms and literary societies. At the Abyssinian Baptist Church, T. McCants Stewart delivered a lecture entitled, "Heredity and Character." '(Clark, p. 101) A.M.E. Zion Church had musical and literary jubilees. While Black churches gave to the needy, they approached it in a haphazard manner; the average Black church failed to fulfill the social needs of the Black masses. Some other important organizations, other than the church, which helped to develop the Black community, were white philanthropic organizations and the public school system. (Clark, p. 92)

The Black church played an important role in the lives of its individual members. The Black man in Harlem experienced feelings of subservience which was imposed on him by his inferior status. He was able to compensate for those feelings in bars, on street corners or in the Black churches. (Clark, p. 174) The Black Church in East Harlem was important to Blacks because it was a social and recreational club and gave them an unhampered opportunity for social life and for exercise of leadership. (Meier, p. 15)

The members, who may have had menial jobs, within the church, could assume greater responsibilities than they could anywhere else. They could engage in politics and financial decisions. It helped develop their self-esteem. If the Black person was the minister, he was permitted a personal freedom and was given presents of cars and clothing. The ministers themselves became a symbol of social and civic success which affected the reputation of their members, through association with them, to be considered influential citizens. (Clark, p. 175)

In order to understand the role of the Black church in Harlem during the Great Depression it is important to understand the historical role of the preacher. The clergymen expressed the Negro point of view in the community. The preacher was the politician, social worker, employment agent and moral counselor of the Negro community. (Clark, pp. 86, 87) In slavery days, when the plantation owner permitted his slaves to participate in religion, he selected the minister. His motive was to control the slaves. The Black minister was projected into being the political as well as the spiritual leader of the Black community. In Harlem it became the rule that if a person needed a job or was arrested, the religious leader was the person to see. This system remained strong during the Depression. (John Henrik Clarke, <u>Harlem a Community in</u> Transition (New York: The Citadel Press, 1964), p. 131)

During the Depression the major churches suffered. It was expensive to keep their great stone churches. Between 1900 and 1920 they committed themselves to large loans which became too much to maintain. They were burdened by mortgages, salaries and upkeep. (Anderson, p. 253)

Many Black ministers were leaders in Black Harlem. (Meier, p. 15) Black clerics had influence in politics, education, social welfare, fraternal organizations and business enterprises; they criticized labor unions and called for civil rights. (Meier, p. 208) Political rallies were held in churches. Clergymen were among the most powerful political leaders. (Meier, p. 130, 131)

The ministers of the 1920's and 1930's were great clergymen in the history of Black Harlem. They were men with extraordinary personalities according to the Herald Tribune in 1930. Some took an interest in public issues and influenced the political choices that their members made. (Anderson, p. 256)

During the Great Depression the Negro church played a big role in Black Harlem. At the beginning of the Depression, Negro churches fed hundreds of unemployed people until the city started a public relief program. Ministers were leaders in economic matters in Harlem. They announced mass labor meetings and notified people of relief programs, jobs and social gatherings. (Ottley, p. 291) Unemployment agencies, shelters and soup kitchens for the needy were run by major churches, like St. Philip's Protestant Episcopal Church and others. (Anderson, p. 243)

In 1930, during the Depression, half of the people depended on unemployment relief. (Anderson, p. 241) The New York Urban League estimated there were over 200,000 Blacks living in Harlem by 1932. In 25 years the Black population in Harlem increased by 600 percent. There were 2 or 3 families living in apartments meant for 1 family. People searched in garbage cans for food. In 1934, over 19,000 Harlem families were on home relief. There were also poor migrants coming from the south, causing tenements to become overcrowded. (Anderson, p. 242)

Some Black churches entered into social welfare activities, such as the Y.M.C.A., and promoted temperance organizations, old folks' homes, orphanages and mutual benefit societies. Some sponsored employment bureaus, industrial classes, slum missions and homes for servant girls.

(Meier, p. 132) The Black church was the foundation of most movements among the Blacks. (Ottley, p. 291)

Pastors of Black churches, once located downtown, followed their congregations to the new Negro neighborhood of Black Harlem. One such pastor was The Reverend Dr. Adam Clayton Powell Sr., who could pass for white. He was tall, well built, handsome and impressive in appearance in a cutaway coat; he encouraged his congregation to move Abyssinian Baptist to Harlem. Adam Clayton Powell, Sr. was born May 5, 1865 and died June 12, 1953. He was the son of a part Black German planter and a mother who was part American Indian. He had only a few years of schooling, worked at odd jobs and lived a carefree immoral life until he was converted in 1885. From 1888 to 1892 he attended Virginia Union University. He graduated from both the theological department and the academic department. He studied law at Howard University and also entered Wayland Theological Seminary in Washington; he studied later at Yale Divinity School and was ordained by Wayland. He then became minister to congregations in Philadelphia and New Haven and arrived in New York in 1908 where he was named pastor of the Abyssinian Baptist Church in December. The congregation was founded one hundred years earlier on Worth Street, then called Anthony Street; it then moved to Thompson Street and Waverly Place, then to West 40th Street. Adam Clayton Powell, Sr. assumed the ministry of the Abyssinian Baptist Church when it was on 40th Street between 7th and 8th Avenues. (Anderson, p. 20) Under Powell's leadership it moved to West 138th Street in Harlem. He enriched his congregation materially and spiritually. He was one of the first Black leaders to buy land in Harlem for the church. He purchased property when the prices were low in 1911. (Kellner, p. 288)

In 1923 a new church building was constructed on 138th Street. The church was designed by a Black architect, Charles W. Bolton. It was built using New York bluestone. The church is a Gothic style edifice with stained glass windows from Europe, peach colored walls, polished wooden pews, an Italian marble baptismal font and a grand organ with pipes two stories high. (Kellner, p. 13) Powell turned the church into a community center, giving aid to needy persons and railed against racism and bad conduct. (Kellner, p. 288)

The militant Adam Clayton Powell (and his son Adam, Jr.), believed that the church was a social center. (Anderson, p. 256) He commented on political events and swayed the audience to his view. He was not afraid to denounce the things with which he did not agree. He called for the social gospel as did other preachers in Harlem. He told his congregation in 1930, that when they clothe men and women, they clothe God. He told them that poor people need more than sympathy and prayers, they need food and clothing. He told them he would give up $1,000 of his salary in the next 3 months to help relieve the unemployment situation. He called on his congregation to donate 5 % of its income in the next 4 months for the same cause and it complied. The Abyssinian Baptist Church, in the first 3 months of 1931, served 28,500 free meals and distributed 525 food baskets, 17,928 pieces of clothing and 2,564 pairs of shoes. (Anderson, p. 243) In 1937, after serving 29 years, Powell retired from the Abyssinian Baptist Church, he was 72 years old. (Anderson, p. 257)

Powell was involved with religious, interracial and civil rights activities. He was founder of the National Urban League and an early leader of the NAACP. He was an organizer of the Silent Protest Parade of 1917 and a proponent of race pride. (Kellner, p. 289) The church became a great political force in Harlem. (Kellner, p. 13)

Adam Clayton Powell, Sr, was a politician who used his church to project programs for the improvement of the community. He dreamed of the day when the church would be a social gospel institution. (Clarke, p. 233)

Clergymen advocated business enterprise among Blacks in Harlem. In 1912, Adam Clayton Powell, Sr., urged members to go into business. He stated that the race could never become rich by saving its money. (Anderson, p. 65) Leaders of the church urged Blacks to open businesses in Harlem to advance themselves and their race. (Anderson, p. 66) Clergymen were clearly advocates of the Puritan ideals of hard work and individual accomplishment.

Black pastors were preoccupied with puritanical values. Rev. Adam Clayton Powell was a moral counselor within the Black community. Powell was a guardian of morality in pre-war Harlem. In 1910 he said that women who were church members were sitting with their feet up on chairs, smoking cigarettes. He declared it was a defilement of pure womanhood and a desecration of sacred motherhood. (Anderson, p. 92) He complained about the notorious red-light district where on Sunday evenings prostitutes solicited worshippers. (Anderson, p. 20) He believed that dancing had a demoralizing effect on the Negro. He complained that the Negro was dancing himself to death. The Tango and the Chicago were destroying "grace and modesty." Many clergymen condemned profanity and lager beer in social gatherings. They said that the purpose of social clubs was pleasure rather than to promote benevolence in the Black community. Their pre-occupation with these values caused the church to fail in resolving many of the races, more pressing, social problems. (Clark, p. 100)

William P. Hayes, of Mt. Olivet Baptist, was another leader in Black Harlem. He was a moral counselor and a political leader. He came close to matching Powell's social gospel gestures. He turned down a salary increase of 400 dollars. (Anderson, p. 257) He criticized civil rights. He used his pulpit to rail against racism and discrimination and advocated a black relationship to the Republican Party. (Anderson, p. 256)

William Lloyd Imes, of St. James Presbyterian, was a partisan of the trade-union movement; George Sims, of Union Baptist could not give money as Powell did. He and others faced their own financial plight. (Anderson, p. 257)

John W. Johnson, of St. Martin's Protestant Episcopal, with Powell, in 1934, led a boycott against department stores that would not hire Black salesman. (Anderson, p. 293) Other important ministers were; Charles Martin of the A.M.E, Frederick Asbury Cullen of Salem Methodist Episcopal Church; William H. Brooks of St. Marks; Marcus Garvey of African Orthodox Church; Ethelred Brown of A.M.E. Zion; C. Ransom, Bishop of A.M.E. Church; Hutchen C. Bishop of Methodist Episcopal Church and M.C. Stachan of Seventh Day Adventist; Hutchens C. Bishop (and his son Shelton), of Saint Philip's Protestant Episcopal; (Anderson, p. 256)

In 1916, Charles Martin was a minister of the African Methodist Episcopal denomination. He was a moral counselor for the Black community. He complained that Blacks in Harlem loved good things, ate and drank too much and were blessed or cursed with optimism. They were caught in a gay life going to saloons. He complained that many were gamblers, pickpockets, pocketbook snatchers, burglars and spurious diamond dealers feeding on hardworking Harlemites. Blacks, he complained, had nothing better to do than to gather on sidewalks around lampposts. (Anderson, p. 99) He complained that Harlem had many preachers without degrees.

He, like other Black ministers, was a critic of civil rights. He stated that the colored man is a soldier marching under a flag that fails to protect him when alive but honors him when dead. (Anderson, p. 100) He was referring to the 15th Regiment of the New York National Guard formed in 1916, with white officers and Black rank and file. (Anderson, p. 101)

Salem Methodist Episcopal Church on W. 53rd street, appointed Frederick Asbury Cullen as minister in 1902. The church relocated in 1924 to 129th street and 7th Avenue in Harlem. (Kellner, p. 89) Its final home became the former Calvary Methodist Episcopal Church. The white people who had worshiped there moved away and the white minister had to sell the church to the incoming Blacks, because of a lack of finances to maintain it. (Osofsky, p. 114)   He served there as minister until 1943 when he retired. He served the community in many secular capacities. Like other Black ministers, Cullen was a leader in the community. He organized the Silent Protest Parade in 1917 and arranged to have the first Afro-American appointed to the New York City police force in 1911. He assisted in organizing the National Urban League, holding its first meeting in his home at St. Nicholas Avenue. (Kellner, p. 90)

Saint Mark's Methodist Episcopal Church was built in 1927 between 137th and 138th streets. The church held elaborate services. Its ceremonies were more important than its sermons and all its participants wore elegant robes, not unlike that of the Roman Catholics. St. Mark's also was a kind of social center. It contained a gymnasium, a swimming pool and rooms for meetings for local organizations. (Kellner, p. 313) Before Powell and Ransom arrived in New York, William H. Brooks was the pastor of St. Mark's who was noted as the city's most politically active Black ministers. He was described by The Colored American, a leading Black magazine in 1906 as an influential, able Afro-American clergyman. He had been minister when the church was located on 53rd Street. (Anderson, p. 24)

African Orthodox Church was formed by Marcus Garvey on 28 September 1921 to end the Blacks subservience to the white God and Christ. Garvey believed Africans should worship a Black God. The Rev. George Alexander McGuire, an Episcopalian minister, gave up his church in 1920 to become the head of the new African Orthodox Church. The church followed Episcopalian and Roman Catholic doctrines except for the Black Madonna, Christ and God. The church was vilified by Black clergymen who accepted a white God. Africans from the Caribbeans, who lived in Harlem, were receptive to the idea of a Black deity. (Kellner, pp. 4, 5)

The Black Baptist denomination was the largest denomination among the Black people in East Harlem, and their preachers were often the leaders in Black communities. Black Baptist congregations, in East Harlem, met in large churches and small storefronts. The churches, in the slum, served as places of stability. They were the centers of hope and celebration, where people could overcome loneliness while having their spiritual needs met.

Blacks adopted and then adapted the Protestant church for their own purposes. Blacks became Baptists because of a born again notion in which God gave people a new start and the promise of liberation. The idea ran parallel with their emancipation to freedom. They seemed to have used this notion in each individual church as each church was free to do things its own way. (Marty, p. 74)

The organized Black church is a great American institution. An example is Mother Zion Church (African Methodist Episcopal Zion), founded in 1796. It was located downtown at Leonard and Church Streets. (Osofsky p. 10) "Mother Zion" Church constructed the Harlem African Methodist Episcopal Zion Church ("Little Zion"). Later in the 20th century, it became an independent church. (Osofsky, p. 83)

African Methodist Episcopal Zion ("Mother Zion") moved uptown. The African Methodist Episcopal Church was founded in 1816. (Claude McKay, Negro Metropolis (New. York: Harcourt Brace Jovanovich, Inc., 1968), p. 74)

Mother Zion's uptown branch called "Little Zion" was in a small wooden building on Harlem's east side for approximately 75 years. They constructed a new church on the west side in 1911. (Osofsky, p. 114)

Bethel African Methodist Episcopal Church (1819) began on Mott Street and moved to the Tenderloin before moving on to Harlem. (Osofsky p. 10) When Rev. C. Ransom, with fair skin and reddish hair, was pastor of the church on West 25th Street he launched a campaign against prostitution. He was a radical Black activist. He said that in the Black Tenderloin he saw human derelicts, moral shipwrecked, degeneracy, vice, ravening wolves and spiritual decay. (Anderson, p. 19) In 1924 he became a bishop of the African Methodist Episcopal Church which was regarded as the most racially militant of all Black religious organizations in America. In 1899 there was a lynching in the deep south, Ranson advised Blacks to become skilled in handling dynamite to use when attacked, for protection of their homes and lives. Ransom would not serve as spiritual adviser to actors and musicians, because they did not lead a moral life style. (Anderson, p. 22) Ransom was appalled to hear that women in Harlem were going to wine parties and smoking cigarettes; he reproved them saying that Black society women were trying to copy what white society women on 5th Avenue were doing. In 1914 women were doing the tango and modern dances. (Anderson, p. 92) Ransom also joined W.E.B. Du Bois in forming the Niagara Movement. (Anderson, p. 22)

St. Philips Protestant Episcopal Church, had one rector from 1886 to 1933, his name was Hutchen C. Bishop. He was bald; light skinned and mild-mannered. St. Philips is, to the present, the wealthiest Black church in the country, reputed as the most exclusive Black church in New York City and was, like many other major churches, engaged in buying Harlem real estate. Its members were considered to be the "best element" in the Black community. Many prominent Blacks, largely mulatto, were its communicants. It was the only Black church in Manhattan with a "Pew System" in the 19th century. In the pew system, members would outbid each other for choice seats in the chapel. St. Philips grew like other important Black Churches. It was founded in Five Points district in 1809. In 1818 it was organized as an offshoot of Trinity Church, in downtown Manhattan. (Anderson, p. 23) It had its first formal meeting in 1819 in a small wooden building on Centre Street. In 1856 it moved to a former Methodist church on Mulberry Street and in 1889 to the Tenderloin at West Twenty-Fifth Street and stayed there until in 1910.   Saint Philip's properties in the Tenderloin were sold by John E. Nail and Henry Parker in 1909. Nail managed the real estate affairs of the church, with which he bought $640,000 worth of Harlem properties.

The money was gained from the sale of its Tenderloin property. (Kellner, p. 73) Then St. Philips moved to a newly constructed church in Harlem. (Osofsky, p. 117) The new building on 133rd Street between 7th and 8th Avenues was built at a cost of $200,000. The parish house became a social center and a stage for the Negro Experimental Theatre in 1931. The church had a large gymnasium, a basketball team, and art classes and during the Depression it was used as a soup kitchen. (Kellner, p. 314)

James W. Brown was a clergyman born 1872 in

North Carolina. He became minister of the Mother Zion African Methodist Episcopal Church, first on 89th Street, then West 136th Street, and in 1925 on W 137th Street. The Rev. Brown was an advocate of social justice; he denounced liquor from the pulpit. (Kellner, p. 56) He spoke out against the desecration of the Sabbath, gambling, pool-playing, improper dancing, moviegoing and selling alcohol. The paper, The Age, said it was a powerful sermon and it too was appalled by the moral laxity in the community. (Anderson, p. 146) Along Lenox Avenue liquor could be obtained in delicatessens, shoe shops, newsstands, stationery stores, soda fountains, cigar stores, and drugstores. Under Prohibition drug stores could prescribe alcohol for their patients so drugstores opened all over Harlem. The ingredients of alcohol called "hooch" were wood alcohol, benzene, kerosene, pyridine, camphor, nicotine, benzol, formaldehyde, iodine, sulphuric acid, soap and glycerin. Harlemites made their own in washtubs, bathtubs, basements, apartment houses; there was little the law or the church could do about it. (Anderson, p. 147)

Seventh Day Adventist Church on W.127th Street had M.C. Strachan as its preacher. Strachan denounced moviegoing from his pulpit along with other churches like the Saints of God in Christ and Sanctified Children of the Holy Ghost. Many different groups of people such as the Black Jews, Black Mohammedans, along with independent spiritualists and preachers in store-front churches spoke out against improper behavior. (Kellner, pp. 73, 74) Illegal drinking caused by Prohibition and carefree behavior such as moviegoing were denounced by Strachan in 1927. Strachan denounced movie houses as "nurseries of vice and seminaries of crime". He said he would expel any church member seen entering of leaving a moving-picture theatre. (Anderson, p. 145)

Factors combined to make Harlem in the 1920's a battleground of intraracial antagonism. There was a settlement of West Indian Blacks in Harlem in the 1920's. West Indians were individuals from Jamaica, Trinidad, Barbados, Martinique, St. Vincent, St. Lucia, Dominica, British Guiana, St. Kitts, Nevis, Montserrat, Antigua, Virgin Islands, Bermuda, the Bahamas, and so on. (Osofsky, p. 132) About 25% of Harlem's population in the twenties was foreign-born. Harlem was America's largest Black melting pot. Although immigration laws of the 1920's restricted the migration of Europeans and excluded Orientals, it had little effect on the peoples of the Caribbean. At first there were no restrictions on West Indian Blacks. After 1924, they entered the country under quotas set aside for their mother countries. Since those quotas were never filled there was a free flow of people from the islands to the U.S. in the 1920's. (Osofsky, p. 131)

There were differences between the Harlemites and the West Indian migrants in the institution of the church. Northern Blacks looked down on the speech and manners of West Indians. Often they glared xenophobically at one another because of their accents and cultural styles.

(Anderson, p. 137) The majority of the Harlemites were Baptists and Methodists. The West Indians were predominantly Episcopalian and Catholic. St. Martins Episcopal Church was founded in Harlem in 1926 for the West Indian immigrants. Services in the immigrant churches were quiet. Sundays were for rest and visiting. Harlemites services were emotional. (Osofsky, p. 134) Black churches, whether major denominations or storefront churches and cult groups, like Father Divine's, played a cathartic role for the Blacks. The leaders provided an opportunity to let off steam, to release their emotions which they could not express safely in their homes or at work. (Clarke, p. 175) The immigrants objected to the "fast ways" of a typical Sunday in Harlem. (Osofsky, p. 134) Pastors did achieve some co-operation as they preached at mass meetings in Harlem churches. (Osofsky, p. 135)

In 1930, according to James Weldon Johnson, there were 160 colored churches in Harlem. He said that 100 of the storefront churches could be closed and there would still be enough of them to serve the Black community. The storefront churches were housed in former candy stores, groceries and shoe-repair shops, basements, lofts and back rooms of tenements. They were an ever-changing group of cults and sects. Preaching was done from rough hewn platforms, music from an upright piano, bass drum and cymbals. Preachers were self-trained, however, many were genuinely devoted to the ethics of their calling, and others were fakers and scoundrels. (Anderson, p. 247) It will be explained later both that Father Divine was genuinely devoted to his calling, although he was very eccentric, and George Becton was a faker and a scoundrel.

There was a real need for storefront churches in Harlem. The people who worshipped there were the least educated and their religious needs were different than the major churches could supply. The traditional liturgy of major churches was not interesting to the storefront worshippers. They wanted an atmosphere conducive to emotional spontaneity. The major churches "were too calm", said Bayard Rustin, a civil rights spokesman who lived in Harlem in the 1930's. People coming from the south were used to screaming, yelling, rolling in the aisles and speaking in tongues, Rustin said. The middle classes, who supported the major churches, were more reverent in church. According to the newspaper, the Age, storefront preachers were listened to and hailed as leaders. The people during the Depression needed their ministers to provide solace or answers to their social and economic problems. (Anderson, p. 248)

Harlem had many cults, mystic chapels and occult shops which can be traced back to Africa, which is a continent of magic practices. The rituals in Northern Africa were extravagant with music, wild dancing and shouting. The fetish gods and the ritual jungle magic of primitive religion could appease their yearnings which were not satisfied *by any* civilized religion. These fetishes were supposed to be in contact with diabolical powers. They could exorcise evil spirits that live in the bodies of human beings. They were often accredited with curing persons with charms, not unlike the Italian Catholic's scapulars, or other magic materials that someone sick may wear around his neck. The occult science in Harlem was similar to the performances of these Guinea fetishes of Africa. They called themselves numerologists, magicians, occultists, metaphysicists, or spiritualists. However, they were West Indian occultists and voodooists. (McKay, pp. 74, 75)

In Harlem they had a more refined appearance. They could be found in basements transformed into mystic chapels where they burn candles, oils and incense. Troubled people went to them for solace, information, job finding, love, friendship, gambling tips or ward off evil, very much as the Italian Catholic beseeched the Madonna for favors and security. Throughout Harlem sacred shops supplied the ritualistic paraphernalia (similar to models of wax organs that the Italian Catholics used in the feast of the Madonna) of occult chapels which have the same appearance as a religious article store; they provide articles for priests and altars. The shelves were loaded with jugs of oils and candles of many colors used in mystic rites of candle lore. The color of the candle is special in meaning. One color (unlike Italian Catholic street theology in which it is the size that matters) might denote a devotion, another color, material gain, self-mastery, power over others, increase love or invoke happiness, communion with the dead, dreams, peace and harmony or ward off evil. Also sold in the sacred shops were herbs, roots and books of numbers. (McKay, p. 76)

There was a high death rate in Harlem, as a study showed from 1923 to 1927 by an Atlanta University professor. Harlem's death rate was 42 % higher than the entire city. Deaths were twice as many at childbirth, infant mortality was 111 per thousand live births; for the city it was 64.5 per thousand. Tuberculosis was 3 times the city rate, pneumonia, heart disease, cancer, rickets, and malnutrition were also very high. (Osofsky, p. 141) Harlem was the most disease ridden community in Manhattan. Many of the causes of Harlem's health problems were a result of the slum environment and poverty. Also, there was a great deal of ignorance among the migrants, both foreign born and native. This led to quackery in the community in the 1920's. This situation allowed "spiritualists", "herb doctors," "African medicine men," " Indian doctors," "dispensers of snake oils," "layers-on-of-hands," "palmists," and "phrenologists" to operate. These quacks promised to cure many illnesses. The ignorance and poverty of the people, along with their superstitious beliefs, hampered real recoveries from physical sicknesses and consequently contributed to the high death rate described above. (Osofsky, p. 143)

Other-healers healed the soul in storefront churches which were founded in Harlem in the 1920's. They preached that Jesus was the doctor, as a sign read hanging over the door to one of those churches. (Osofsky, p. 145) The Saturday Evening Post said in 1925, that Harlem has dozens of varieties of doctors, proclaiming schools of medicine that probably do not exist anywhere else in the world. The Survey Graphic said that "the Black art flourishes in Harlem". Feats of witchcraft were done daily. A well known drug store on Lenox Avenue sold roots, herbs, bark from trees, in curled form, in powder form and in spiral bunches; they sold cures for various illnesses. (Anderson, p. 149) There were 140 Black churches in a 150 block area of Harlem in 1926. Only 54 churches were in magnificent and costly church buildings. The rest were in stores and homes and they appealed to the least educated people of Harlem. They were self appointed pastors called "Jack-leg preachers," "cotton-field preacher," who preached to all who would listen. The nondenominational sects took the meager worldly goods from their members as contributions and preached that Satan and terror was everywhere. One pastor said that the devil runs every theatre. (Osofsky, p. 144) Services were loud; members felt the spirit of the Lord, shouted and begged for His forgiveness. Tambourines heightened the emotionalism to a state of frenzy. Although most storefront preachers were probably charlatans, there was an exception. The Reverend Mr. R.C. Lawson in 1919 founded the Church of Christ, Apostolic Faith, of Louisiana. He decried the lack of emotionalism in the established urban churches. He complained that the Black congregations were copying "the white man's style," he said; he offered the migrants fire and brimstone of religious services in the rural south. (Osofsky, p. 145) By 1930 the Apostolic Church had forty branches throughout the country.

It is important to explore cults and occults so they can be compared to the primitive religions of the traditional Jew, Catholic and especially the Italian Catholics with their street theology and cult of the Madonna. There is a difference between occultists and cultists. Cultists followed the tradition of the prophets whereas Harlem's occultists were descendants of fetish priests. The occultists dressed and decorated their altars in pagan and Christian symbols. They wore oriental vestments, either Hindu, Persian, Arabian or Egyptian. Devotees of the occult listened to a rosary of meaningless words from the dead or have dreams interpreted. Perhaps not unlike Italian Catholics they were like drug addicts coming for a fix. (McKay, p. 76) One prominent occultist in Harlem was the wife of the cult leader George Wilson Becton--Madame Josephine Becton. (McKay, p. 79) People who were devoted to the occult found spiritual comfort in colorful dim lit atmospheres and experienced the same solace as those who went to the shrine of a great cathedral. (McKay, p. 81)

The occult is anything pertaining to, or concerned with alchemy, magic, astrology and other arts or practices involving use of divination, incantation (a parallel of Judao-Christian prayer) or a magical formula. It is beyond the scope or understanding and hidden from sight. It is transcendent of the natural. It is supernatural in essence. Occultism is the belief in hidden or mysterious powers and the possibility of human control over them. (Merriam-Webster, Webster's New Collegiate Dictionary (Massachusetts: G. & C. Merriam Co., Publishers, 1961) Some Blacks in East Harlem were occultist. The Negro loved religion and, being human, was subject to rights of animism. Veneration of the saints, as shown in Italian Catholic street theology, is similar to the ritualistic religion of the occult in East Harlem. It was therefore no less hateful and disgusting to many nativists who were more steeped in science than in animism or superstition.

A cult is a system of deity worship, a great devotion to some idea or a living religious leader, a new teaching, or an unusual occult practice. It is not unlike the Italian Catholic's devotion to the cult of the Madonna. A cult may consist of a few followers or a worldwide organization which generally would not refer to itself as a cult and would even reject the term. It may be a new religious movement. Most leaders of cults demand that the members live apart from society in a commune, as in the case of George "Father Divine" Baker. The leaders claim to have exclusive religious truth and they want absolute obedience and allegiance from their followers. Cults often require that the members contribute all their possessions to the group. The cultist is the devotee or practitioner of a cult. (Merriam-Webster Dictionary)

The occult religion of some Blacks, many of whom

were foreign born, exceeded the confines of the Protestant church. It may be considered a cult because it was immersed in African magic.

Cults were always numerous in Harlem. The Black church let its people and preachers prompt the congregations to shout and stomp of the old-time religion. Many cultists used banjos and tambourines in their performances on sidewalks. Many shouted from basements and abandoned stores. They were tolerated by ordained ministers who did not take them seriously, but found them humorous. Ministers, intellectuals, along with church-goers, thought the cults were local circuses, not unlike the Irish and German Catholic attitude toward the Italian Catholic's street theology. (McKay, p. 82) Two cults in Harlem were the World's Gospel Feast, founded by George Becton and the Peace Mission, founded by Father Divine. (McKay, p. 83)

During the 1930's the great cult leaders of Harlem were evangelists George W. Becton and Father Divine. Although the average storefront had a membership of about 50, Becton and divine, both had thousands of members that extended beyond Harlem and New York and they were not limited to storefront churches. Becton preached in major churches and Divine had brownstones, which were owned or rented. They were both colorful, dramatic, influential figures and were almost as rich as the major churches. (Anderson, p. 248)

Elder (George Wilson) Becton was an evangelist and

cult leader in East Harlem. He was an example of a faker and a scoundrel that existed in Harlem during the 1930's. He lived form 1890 to 1933. He was born in Texas. He was tall, handsome and well built. He wore tailored clothes, a top hat, and ivory gloves and carried a cane. (Anderson, p. 249) Becton had a cook, valet and a chauffeur. He was aloof, and was worshipped by his followers. (McKay, p. 85) His style of preaching and physical movements on the platform caused him to be nicknamed the Dancing Evangelist. In 1922 he came to Harlem as president of the World Gospel Feast Party, Inc.; its quarterly publication, the "Menu", offered "A Square Deal for God". (Anderson, p. 249) However, Becton was more interested in collecting donations than souls. He bought property in Harlem with the parishioner's contributions of 70 cents per week. Becton had 200,000 followers. (Kellner, p. 30)

George Wilson Becton was the first of the great cult leaders who stirred the Harlem community in the beginning of the 1930's. Becton began his cult with 12 young disciples and an orchestra. He was college educated as opposed to most Harlem cultists at that time who were all illiterates; this enabled him to speak the language of the educated Blacks. His meetings were orderly. There was music playing and pages wore beautiful robes. The congregation swayed with the music and sang gospel hymns. Becton was an inspiring preacher that ordained ministers invited to their pulpits. He was called to preach at the Salem Methodist Episcopal Church, by its pastor Rev.

F.E. Cullen, to provide spiritual excitement. (McKay, p. 84)

Becton asked his congregation to give dimes to the church collection instead of using them to gamble. His congregation complied and Becton became wealthy purchasing two houses, one apartment and a golden bed with gold slippers. He had a golden gate which led from an immense music room and reception room into his private rooms, which he called his holy chambers. His bathroom was decorated luxuriously with bazaar oriental cushions. He sometimes dined there. (McKay, p. 84) He advocated celibacy as Father Divine did later. He was kidnapped by two white men and shot. Father Divine then formed his Kingdom of Peace. (McKay, p. 85)

In contrast to George Wilson Becton, was a devoted, but eccentric cult leader named Father Divine. George, Father Divine Baker was a cult leader who lived from 1880 to 1965. Father Divine, like other preachers in Harlem, was a politician, a social worker, an employment agent and a moral counselor. He was considered to be God by his followers. He raised the hopes of Blacks by presenting himself as a Black God who would bring peace and plenty, respect and brotherhood to people, who at the time in East Harlem, were experiencing racism and the Great Depression. (Kellner, p. 27) He came from the south and preached in Sayville, Long Island, about peace, brotherhood, cleanliness, and honesty from 1919-1931. Divine's congregation, in 1931, was cited for being a nuisance by citizens of Sayville, because of wild stamping, shouting and dancing. His words were like a magic potion. Strange phrases mixed with advice on daily living were spiritual nourishment for his thousands of followers. (McKay, p. 36) Father Divine was arrested, tried and sentenced. He was released after the judge died. His fanatical followers believed that the judge was punished for opposing Father Divine and the incident transformed him into a supreme being to thousands of people. His cult was different from others because no contributions were solicited. The mystery as to where he got the money caused publicity, which in turn, increased contributions to him and gave the public the impression that he had a supernatural power to create money. (McKay, p. 33) He had come to the people to free them from tyranny, segregation and hunger. He expected and received loyalty from his followers. In return he gave his members housing, employment, food and clothing. He moved his mission to Harlem in 1933. Divine, in the role of a social worker devised a plan for co-operative housing where lodgers received free room and board. Tasks were performed by those not employed, while those employed supplied the necessities. (McKay, p. 34) He imposed celibacy on his disciples. (McKay, p. 38).

Even before moving to Harlem, Divine was a provider for his followers. He found them jobs and gave them lodging in his headquarters of Sayville and invited them regularly to magnificent banquets--offering them free jobs, free housing and free food. He always had money, and to explain all this, he told his followers that "God will provide". (Anderson, p. 251) In Harlem in 1932, Father Divine was a moral counselor; during his sermons he called on his followers to eschew smoking, drinking, crime, violence, race hatred, profane language, hair straightening, installment buying and sex. His organization also ran many small stores.

Some major churches were in opposition to Divine. Clergyman R.C. Lawson denounced the Father's claim to divinity as "a sham and a delusion", as he spoke to fellow clergymen. Father Divine was harassed by his enemies and lawsuits concerning his property. He moved to Philadelphia in the early 1940's leaving a vacuum in Harlem filled by superstar evangelists, such as Elder Lightfoot Michauu, Mother Horn and Sweet Daddy Grace. (Anderson, p. 253)

Some early conflicts in Harlem involved controversies over such things as control of church property, religious teaching in the schools and issues of separation between the church and state. The Protestants were suspicious of the Roman Catholic Church in Harlem. (Dinnerstein, p. 37) Italian Catholics were confronted by hatred. Anti-Catholicism came from the first English Protestants who settled in America in the 17th century. They were products of the Reformation; they regarded the Pope as a foreign tyrant with international influence. In 1885, Josiah Strong wrote, " Our Country: Its Possible Future and Its Present Crisis". Strong argued that papal principles were not conducive to principles of free institutions. Therefore, papal principles were a threat to American institutions. (Alan M. Kraut, <u>The Immigrant in American Society. 1880-1921</u> (Illinois: Harlan Davidson, Inc., 1986), p. 154) Protestants believed that the Irish and German Catholics established parochial schools to preserve their old traditions and thwart assimilation. (Dinnerstein, p. 37)

Wealthy executive Protestants led the reform movement in the Protestant churches in Harlem. They accepted the theory of evolution and liberalized religious thought; embracing the social gospel they began an unprecedented movement for social reform in the city. (Rischin, p. 197) The immigrants arriving in Harlem who were in need of advice or assistance were dependent upon private charities which were supported by ethnic or religious institutions or philanthropists. It was shown above that assistance was offered from welfare organizations established by Protestant reformers who were inspired by the Social Gospel movement or other assimilated members of an ethnic group who hoped to aid the immigrants in making a transition into the American culture. Protestant Social Gospel reformers established libraries, gymnasiums, soup kitchens, clinics, employment offices, YMCA and the YWCA. The Salvation Army provided services such as emergency food, shelter, health services, and rescue missions for prostitutes, unwed mothers, alcoholics and instructional facilities in many subject areas. (Kraut, p. 127)

The book explained that many of the social welfare programs designed for the immigrants were actually missionary efforts in disguise. Such programs alienated many immigrants especially of Roman Catholic or Jewish faiths. Protestants wanted these immigrants to abandon their past and give up old world habits, customs and native languages. Protestant reformers feared that a culturally pluralistic society would destroy American democracy. The religions and values of these groups were considered primitive as compared to progressive Protestant Christianity. (Kraut, p. 128)

In contrast to the Italians the Jews were able to unite for community action. Jews helped their brethren in distress. They organized defense organizations like B'nai B'rith's Anti-Defamation League. They pledged to protect the civil rights of all the Jews throughout the world. (Dinnerstein, p. 57) The Jewish faith made charity a social obligation, and no matter how loose the formal religious bonds became, most Jews regarded philanthropic activities as an absolute necessity. Through it, they were honored within the Jewish community of Harlem and elsewhere. (Dinnerstein, p. 57) It was shown that the Jews in Harlem through philanthropic activity helped their coreligionists. German or Americanized Jews aided the East European Jews when they came to Harlem. They acted out of noblesse oblige and fear that the East European Jews might become a burden to society and intensify the existing anti-Semitism. They established educational institutions, orphanages, and homes for unwed mothers, recreational facilities and hospitals. They developed the Jewish Theological Seminary to train Americanized rabbis to help Jewish immigrants become Americanized. (Dinnerstein, p. 58) The Jews differed from the Italians. In order for the Italians to be considered more American they were expected to be more observant of their formal religious doctrines. The Jews, on the other hand, were religiously observant. In order for them to become Americanized they had to weaken, rather than strengthen, their religious ties. (Dinnerstein, p. 57) East European Jews experienced anti-Semitism based on the orthodox Christian view of Jews as being God's Chosen People who betrayed their Lord. Goldwin Smith, a distinguished historian at Cornell University, contributed to anti-Semitism. He said the Jews are a parasitic race who preserves their tribalism and tribal interests. Therefore, they should not have a right to share political power in a community to which they did not belong. (Kraut, p. 155)

The book has explained that the southern Italian's attitude toward religion differed from most Americans and other immigrants. Therefore, they were a threat to the Protestant values and interests. The Irish and German Catholics were dedicated to the faith; they respected the institution of the church, whereas the Italians, out of resentment of the Irish dominations, regarded the Church as cold and almost puritanical. The Italians viewed priests as being lazy and ignorant who lived off the community.

They did not attend regular church services. Out of 50,000 Italians in New York City in 1864, 48,800 neglected church services. The Italians did not adhere to the doctrine and were ignorant of many traditional aspects of Roman Catholicism. They were more devoted to festivals and fiestas, which, to them, were more significant than the formal church services. The Italians, unlike the many Protestants, were steeped in superstition. They feared the evil-eye and through rituals, symbols and charms they warded off evil spirits and gained support from powerful deities. (Dinnerstein, p. 56)

The Italians were also unable to unite for community action. Southern Italians were devoted to their families and members of their own villages; they lacked overall ethnic commitment. They were divided by dialects, thought and life-styles, making group organization almost impossible in the United States. (Dinnerstein, p. 57) However, as was shown earlier, their devotion to the Madonna had the affect of solidifying the people of East Harlem into an Italian community.

Blacks differed from European immigrant groups because they were not clannish, they did not have the same close family ties which other groups created and used for professional and business advancement. Blacks did not have a special language and culture or a history of experience that would have created a morale, which could have lead them to build a life of their own. The Black church was an exception to this. The Black church, for the Black member, functioned like the clans of Jews and the extended Italian families. The preachers were able to lead their congregations to a better life in Harlem. The Church provided for professional and business advancement. It was the Black preacher within the institution of the church who provided influence in politics, education, social welfare, fraternal organizations and business enterprises. It was perhaps not an accident that the tight church groups among Blacks have often branched out in business, as was the case of Father Divine's cult. Preachers were the moral counselors that provided a new tradition among the Blacks which gave them the solace that other groups found in their old traditional orders which they transformed and developed in East Harlem, between 1880 and 1935. (Glazer, p. 33)

The following conclusions can be drawn from this essay. In the old traditional orders of the Jews, Italians and Blacks, the people created rational standards for themselves which they accepted. The standards were designed to keep a hierarchy of order among the members of the group. It was through the traditional order that each individual learn his position and the duties which he had to fulfill in the hierarchy. Every member of the group was supported by all the other members, both seen and unseen. (Stephen Neill, Christian Faith & Other Faiths (Illinois: Intervarsity Press, 1984), p. 172)

In East Harlem, between 1880 and 1935, it has been shown that there were forces of disintegration that broke up the older orders that had affected the lives of both societies and individuals. One factor was the growth of cities which act like magnets drawing in people as they tried to fulfill their hopes. The breakup of the old order resulted in the emergence of the individual as an entity. This was a break from the old traditional order where everything fell into a pattern; occasions for personal decisions were few and far between. Even marriage, in the old traditional orders, was the decision of parents or elders of the community instead of the boy and girl concerned. (Neill p. 175)

When the Jews, Italians or Blacks entered Harlem they lived among groups of their own people. However, it has been shown that in the modern environment the old familiar rules seemed to be inapplicable. At home everything was shared, but in Harlem individual possession was the rule. Once the individual was accustomed to the freer kind of existence he was no longer able to operate within the old restrictions and he could not continue to accept with docility what his elders demanded. (Neill, p. 175, 176)

Another characteristic that was found to exist in the broken traditional structures discussed earlier was that there were two types of aristocracies which were in conflict. One was concerned with the old hierarchy which had at the head a learned rabbi among the Jews or the central women among the Italians. The other type of aristocracy depended not on heredity, but on the individual's ability to learn as an individual, thereby, acquiring knowledge and power outside of the traditional educational system. (Neill, p. 176)

Another problem arose from the breakup of the traditional order, namely, a loss of identity. The individual became perplexed within the new environment. (Neill, p. 177) There was a strong pull of the old simpler, idealized life of the past. In the traditional system the individual learned the law, which had to be kept. If the law was broken all his people would be punished. This system created a conscience in the person being educated. It was shown to exist in the Jewish and Italian traditional orders. (Neill, p. 178) The essay alludes to the notion that a man is by nature religious. If his present religion does not satisfy him, he will create one that does. (Neill, p. 179) It does not seem possible for a person to be satisfied with mere materialism. The events which took place in Harlem showed that the change in the social and economic order was accompanied by a felt need for a new religion and the Jews, Italians and Blacks responded accordingly. (Neill, p. 181)

Bibliography

Anderson, Jervis. This Was Harlem. New York: Farrar
Straus Giroux, 1982.

Antin, Mary. The Promised Land. New Jersey: Princeton
University Press, 1985.

Amfitheatrof, Erik. The Children of Columbus. Boston:
Little Brown and Company, 1973.

Bayor, Ronald. Neighbors in Conflict. Chicago: University
of Illinois Press, 1988.

Birmingham, Stephen. The Rest Of Us. Massachusetts:
Little, Brown and Company, 1984.

Bodnar, John. The Transplanted. Bloomington: Indiana
University Press, 1985.

Sauer, Jerald C. Protestantism in America. Pennsylvania:
The Westminster Press, 1965.

Clark, Kenneth B. Dark Ghetto. New York: Harper &
Row Publishers, 1965.

Clarke, John Henrik. Harlem a Community in Transition.

.New York: The Citadel Press, 1964.

Connolly, Charles. What Is The Church For?. New York.:
Scepter Publishers, 1979.

Dinnerstein, Leonard & David M. Reimers. Ethnic
Americans. New York: Harper & Row, Publishers, 1988.

Einstein, Stephen J. and Lydian Kukoff. Every Person's
Guide to Judaism. New York: UAHC Press, 1989.

Feldstein, Stanley. The Land That I Show You. New York:
Anchor Press/Doubleday, 1979..

Fishbane, Michael. Judaism. San Francisco: Harper &
Row, Publishers, 1987.

Foy, Felician A. Catholic Almanac. Indiana: Our Sunday
Visitor, Inc., 1990.

Fredrickson, George M. The Black Image in the White
Mind. New York: Harper & Row, Publishers., 1971.

Gabaccia, Donna R. From Sicily to Elizabeth Street.
Albany: State University of New York Press, 1984.

Gambino, Richard. Blood Of My Blood. New York:
Doubleday & Company, Inc., 1974.

Glazer, Nathan & Daniel Patrick Moynihan. Beyond The
Melting Pot. Massachusetts: The M.I.T. Press, 1963.

Golden, Harry. A Bintel Brief. New York: Ballantine
Books, 1971.

Greenberg, Irving. The Jewish Way. New York: Summit
Books, 1988.

Gurock, Jeffrey 6. When Harlem Was Jewish. 1870-1939.
New York: Columbia -University Press, 1979.

Haller, John S. Outcasts From Evolution. Chicago:
University of Illinois Press, 1971.

Halliburton, Warren J. and Ernest Kaiser. Harlem. New
York: Doubleday & Company Inc., 1974.

Hapgood, Hutchins. The Spirit of the Ghetto.
Massachusetts: Harvard University Press, 1967.

Hardon, John A., S.J. The Catholic Catechism. New York:
Doubleday and Company, 1975.

Harris, Lis. Holy Days: The World of a Hasidic Family.

New York: Summit Books, 1985.

Higham, John. <u>Strangers In The Land.</u> New York:

Atheneum, 1970.

Howe, Irving, <u>World of Our Fathers.</u> New York: Simon &

Schuster, Inc., 1976.

Joselit, Jenna Weissman. <u>Our Gang.</u> Bloomington: Indiana

University Press, 1983.

Kellner, Bruce ed. <u>The Harlem Renaissance.</u>

Connecticut: Greenwood Press, Inc., 1984.

Kessner, Thomas. <u>The Golden Door.</u> New York: Oxford

University Press, 1977.

Kraut, Alan M. The Huddled Masses: The Immigrant in

American Society, 1880-1921. Illinois:. Harlan Davidson,

Inc., 1986.

Lawson, E. Thomas. <u>Religions of Africa.</u> San Francisco:

Harper and Row, Publishers, 1984.

Lopreato, Joseph. <u>Italian Americans.</u> New York: Random

House Inc., 1970.

Neill, Stephen. <u>Christian Faith & Other Faiths.</u> Illinois:

Intervarsity Press, 1984.-

Noss, John B. David S. Noss. <u>Man's Religions.</u> New York: Macmillian Publishing Company, 1984.

Marty, Martin E. <u>Christian Churches in the United States.</u> New York: Harper & Row,-Publishers, Inc., 1987.

McKay, Claude. <u>Harlem: Negro Metropolis.</u> New York: Harcourt Brace Jovanovich, Inc., 1968.

McPherson, James M. <u>The Abolitionist Legacy.</u> New Jersey: Princeton University Press, 1975.

Meier, August. <u>Negro Thought in America. 1880-1915.</u> Ann Arbor: The University Michigan Press, 1969.

Melton, J. Gordon. Encyclopedic Handbook of Cults in America. New York & London: Garland Publishing Inc., 1986.

Merriam-Webster. <u>Webster's New Collegiate Dictionary.</u> Massachusetts: G. & C. Merriam Co., Publishers, 1961.

Orsi, Robert Anthony. <u>The Madonna of 115th Street.</u> New Haven: Yale University Press, 1985.

Osofsky, Gilbert. Harlem: The Making of a Ghetto, 1890-

1930. New York: Harper & Row, Publishers, Inc., 1966.

Ottley, Roi and William J. Weatherby. The Negro in New York. New York: Oceana Publications, Inc., 1967.

Painter, Nell Irvin. Exodusters. New York: Alfred A. Knopf, Inc., 1977.

Peebles, Robert Whitney. Leonard Covello: A Study of Immigrant's Contribution to N.Y.C. Volume I. New York: New York University, 1967.

Ploski, Harry A. ed. The Negro Almanac African American. New York: Gale Research Inc., 1989.

Ray, Benjamin. African Religions. New Jersey: Prentice-Hall, Inc., 1976.

Rischin, Moses. The Promised City. Massachusetts: Harvard University Press, 1962.

Rolle, Andrew. The Italian Americans. Oklahoma: University of Oklahoma Press, 1980.

Scheiner, Seth M. Negro Mecca. New York: New York University Press, 1965

Schoener, Allon. Portal To America: The Lower East Side,

1870-1925. New York: Holt, Rinehart and Winston, 1967.

Steinberg, Stephen. The Ethnic Myth. Boston: Beacon

Press, 1978.

Stern, Zelda. Ethnic New York. New York: St. Martins -

Press, Inc., 1980.

Wiebe, Robert H. The Search For Order. 1877-1820. New

York: Hill and Wang, 1967.

www.ingramcontent.com/pod-product-compliance
Lightning Source LLC
Chambersburg PA
CBHW070116290526
45789CB00005B/2038